African Yesterdays
and Other Horizons

ISBN 978-1-5272-8735-8

Website: www.southdevonwriter.co.uk
Facebook page: @bulawayotodevon
Published by Cyndi Barker
Original lino prints by Cyndi Barker
Cover design and layout by Audra Bouwer
Printed by Short Run Press Limited, Exeter, UK

African Yesterdays
and Other Horizons

A COLLECTION OF POETRY

Cyndi Barker

To those I'm fondest of,
especially Michael and Henry,
my heart's delights.

Preface

I started writing poetry as a way of expressing my innermost turmoil.

It was three in the morning and I was sitting on the carpet in a small bedsit in England, alone, after my family had gone their separate ways. I was feeling homesick and pondering where it had all gone wrong.

As the tears started to fall, I picked up my phone and started to record how I was feeling. The poems in this collection are the result.

The first poem I put on social media was "I Wanted to Grow Old in Africa." I was overwhelmed by the response it received from people all over the world. People reaching out to tell me their stories and how my poem had touched their lives. It was a great comfort to me to know other people were feeling the same. Suddenly, I didn't feel so alone anymore and writing poetry became my therapy while I tried to figure it all out.

I would like to thank all the people who have connected with me from across the miles and for all the kind comments and support I have received. They have become real friends and I have met some of them too. I was delighted to find Donna, whilst on holiday in Mykonos, who was born in Devon and had spent her childhood in Zimbabwe!

I would also like to thank everyone who made this collection possible: Audra for her unfaltering assistance with cover design and typesetting – she's more like an angel than a sister; Tim for designing and maintaining my website; Di Nicholls who helped me to write the bit on the back cover and who listened without prejudice; Ro, Netta and Darrell for all their patience; and finally, to all my muses who bore it well!

I am truly humbled and very grateful to you all. From an African poet travelled to Devon to find her soul.

Cyndi Barker
March 2021

Contents

Preface   *vi*

African Yesterdays   *1*

I wanted to grow old in Africa   2
Open love letter to Zimbabwe   4
In the midst of the Victoria Falls   7
Townsend High School - Bulawayo   10
A little bottle of soil   14
The old house on Matopos Road   16
Dare we hope   19
There'll be parties in the old country tonight   20
Sound the gong   22
In quieter moments   24
We left before the jacaranda season   26
Where the flame lilies grow   28
It came to me in a dream last night   31
A long time ago   34
Once upon a time a girl from Africa   36
The house in Greendale   38
Falling blossoms of the jacaranda tree   41
The story of a crocodile   43
A piece of clay   46
In a country nestled between two rivers   48
There's something about eating a mango   52
My life is like an upside-down snow globe   54
Restful respite   57
A rhino's last tears   59
I am a princess   62
Just another day   65

Homeland   67
Girl from Gubulawayo   70
World's View   72
The smell of the rain   74
Cosmos by the railway line   76
Africa calling   78
A child and his grandfather   80
Just a dream away   82
African   84
Prayer for Zimbabwe   86
Oliver   88
One foot in front of the other   90
A place called home   92
Justice for Zimbabwe   94
Of dust and dreams   96
A letter of love to my birth country   98
African child with feet in sand   101
The first rains   104
Beggars and exiles   106
Rosen   109

Devonshire   *113*
Blessed Easter Sunday   114
Up on the moors   115
On the train again   118
I often visit Tor Cross in my dreams   119
A rain-washed night in Devon   121
Scene from a west Charleton window   123
On arrival   124
Autumn English roses   127
Grey around the bay   130

Crazy, carefree, young things 132
Royal wedding 134
A January morning in South Devon 137
To Devonshire with love 139
For Leia 142
Once upon an English May morn 144
The last day of August 145
Reflections on a wet August morn 146
These four walls 148
The birds have flown south 150
A call to war 152
He sat on the foreshore alone 155
How beautiful Devonshire looks in the sunshine! 157
Summer has given us the slip! 159
My bridge 161
Someone to share the view 163
Just another half an hour 165
The hotel of dead bats 167
Salcombe meandering 168

Matters of the Heart

171
The unobtainable rose 172
Wistful love 174
The Southern African Lonely Hearts Club 175
I met him when I was seventeen 177
The butterfly in the room 180
You stole into my thoughts today 182
Broken valentine 184
Can I help it? 186
It's always this time of the year 188
I woke up this morning with sunshine in my heart 190

Oh, please be mine   192

Why do we always want what we cannot have?   196

A perfect dream   198

Desire   200

What if I found you at my door?   202

He took my hand   204

Slow dancing to Tina Turner   206

If kisses were wishes   208

Passion is ...   210

An ordinary Friday   212

Oh, my far and distant love   214

In Avonlea did I lay my head   216

We met after an absence of ten or so years   218

It started with a song   221

Looking for my Mr Darcy   223

For it is written   225

He slipped into my life when I wasn't looking   227

Reminisces of a quixotic soul   230

It was just one afternoon a long time ago   232

I wonder if he likes strawberry jam?   235

On reflection   237

An exercise in irony   239

The dangerous addictive nature of dark chocolate   242

Naughty little Cupid   244

The couple at the end of the jetty   246

Love knows   248

Love gone wrong song   250

The other brother   252

His song   254

She   256

If ever I marry again   259

Moon over Bowcombe   261
For DJG   262
On church steps   265
I believe in romance   267

Yesterday, Today and Tomorrow   *269*
Suspended in time   270
On the death of Leonard Cohen   273
The perfect happiness of a tomato sandwich   275
A mother's lament (and fathers too for that matter!)   277
The weather was warm   278
Love from a distance   281
Conversations with the dead   284
On the passing of Hugh Masekela   287
For my son   290
Two sisters   293
On Women's Day   295
The good ole boys of Klipdrift   297
I know I don't say it enough   300
These four little buttons   303
The child on the veranda   305
There is no concept of time in the land of darkness   308
In loving memory of my mother   310
As we pass the 18th door   312
My mother's eyes   316
The little things we collect   318
Departing of a friend   321
For the love of a lad   323
The keeper of memories   325
For Tilly   327
Green eyes   330

Soft-spoken words   333
The old love letter   335
The silk scarf   337
From now until then   339
Beginning   340
My guardian grandad   342
The old bedroom   345

Other Horizons   *347*

Dreams of sand   348
Thoughts from abroad   349
40 degrees in Marrakesh   350
In the shadow of the mosque we wandered   352
Seven days in Marrakesh   353
Wedding in Mijas   356
The lone saxophonist of Mykonos   358
With love from Mykonos   359
Travel the world they say   361
From a veranda in Mykonos   364
Greek Independence Day   366
Farewell to this fair Grecian Isle   368
As the weary travellers make their way home   371
Travellers   373

Inspirational   *375*

The people in my head have gone to bed   376
Clear your mind and relax   378
Never waste a word   380
We tell our stories   382
Wrong turns can be the best turns   384
Thoughts at three   386

As we look forward to the New Year   388

The poet at Christmas (2017)   391

It's the last day of the year   394

Rise above the mundane   396

In my heart   399

In the company of trees   401

Someone sent me a heart today   403

Blow out the candle and come to bed   405

They say you shouldn't dwell in the past   407

I won't let booze numb the pain   409

Oh, how temporary is the beauty of the moment   411

Freedom   413

There are some days   416

The butterfly and the bumble bee   418

Sitting on the step   420

Painting fields yellow   422

Almost perfection   424

Just look up   426

Pink Gin summer   428

Dear Lord   430

The broken vase   432

Journey's end   434

Ground Zero   437

A closing note   438

1

African Yesterdays

I wanted to grow old in Africa

I wanted to grow old in Africa
With the sun warming my decrepit bones
And my great grandchildren running through my grapevine
The heat of the sun turning their skins bronze
While they played in the sprinkler like I had done many
summers ago
Sweet potatoes dug up for tea
Mangoes and pawpaws ripening in the sun
Cicadas in the trees
Nyama in the pot
Sitting on the veranda watching dusk creep up on me
Cloaked in that velvet warm darkness.
Respected for my wisdom
Revered for my vision and experience
And my son would offer me his arm and my daughter would
come for advice
And I would smile and tell them how it was when I was young
And as the embers burn low
In the grate of life
I would willingly walk to the end of the path
Look over the gate to the other side
And know when I am gone
My heart will be buried in the soil
Deep in the land where I was born
And I would be content to be married to elements that bring
new life to the grass
And when the wind blows among the *kopjes* my spirit will
wander there once more.
If we end where we begin

Why am I so far away, trapped between two hemispheres
as I walk and wander and toil away my years?
The dark days are upon us again in the north
Bringing with them who knows what
Soon the cold will descend and my eyes will grow heavy from the strain of the gloom
I will shiver and curse the grey in the sky
As my neighbours shut their doors against it
I will dream of the burning sun and remember the halcyon days of my youth
Where the endless sky stretched forever
It was my blue print for life
My beginning, everything I knew.
Sentimental am I
Nostalgic for times passed
And a land that exists no more
It is true.
For those cynics who call me foolish
I tell you this
You will only miss something once you no longer have it
and no one can understand that pain in your heart,
That longing, until they know what it means to be displaced
So please leave me to my dreams
To my memories
But most of all to my wish.
Yes, I wanted to grow old in Africa,
but life had other horizons for me to pursue.
Other things for me to do.

Open love letter to Zimbabwe

I cried for you today
And as the tears spilled down my cheeks
I thought of your warm smiles and open hearts
and how your mothers nurtured me
And the countless children they carried on their backs
And the sunshine waking us up every morning
And how we thought we'd be in our home forever
Never imagining for one moment that we would leave of our own
free will
Thinking we would be fine elsewhere
And that Africa and its politics could go and hang for all we cared
And we moved away and boarded planes
And we set up camp
In the far flung corners of the planet
And we barbecued our *boerewors* on Australian beaches
And celebrated American independence
And wrapped ourselves in blankets against the UK winters
Learnt new languages and borrowed other people's cultures.
But one African will soon seek out another
No matter whether they be in the Netherlands or Ireland
And we soon flocked together
Made batches of sticky *koeksusters*
And were frowned upon with our raw meat eating habits by our
pasty faced neighbours and we too lost our colour
As our vibrancy slipped from us.
And we danced to our Johnny Clegg and Mango Groove to
remember our happiness
and called each other *"shamwari"*
And slipped into Sindebele and Shona greetings and *"yebo gogos"*

and *"tatendas"* whenever we met

And we remembered we were not English, Australian or American

No, we are Africans and we are too far away from home

Far from the lazy Limpopo, the mozzies in our ears at night

The blackjacks in our socks and the go-away birds

The blue fish eagles and a Kariba sunset

And we're miles away from the mists of Nyanga

And the roar of the mighty Falls and the Zambezi that runs through us as blue as our veins as surely as we ran through the rain forest as children

While our parents sipped G&Ts on the vast veranda of the Vic Falls Hotel

And our hearts wept and broke when we realised that our childhood was a lifetime away

And we are not okay after all

We were lost and we had left our souls in the land of our birth

Mine is in the Matopos somewhere among the balancing rocks.

How I wish we had something to celebrate as we turn another corner on the 18th day of April every year

But our visionaries are all gone

And our expectations have vanished in the dust of 40 years.

Now all we can do is pray for deliverance

And hope our memories last long enough for us to share them with our children

Who will never know the inheritance we wanted to pass on to them.

This will only live on in our stories and faded photographs

And as we wipe away those tears

And wonderful years

We give thanks for those golden savannah summers in the burnt bushveld

For the love of a million mothers and for fathers who threw us
up on their shoulders and pushed us in wheelbarrows
And our childhood companions,
brothers and sisters from different mothers who we knew before
we knew what different colours we were.
Ngiyabonga, *Tatenda* from all your children
We are who we are
because of you gave us a happy and loved childhood
And in our dreams we return
Every night and walk where our foot prints have blown away
Although we are no longer there
You reside in our hearts, in our minds
In our identity
For how can a child forget their parent?
I pray for the starving children
And the mothers with AIDS
And the fathers who cannot save their babies dying in their arms
I will never stop longing for peace in Zimbabwe
And hoping for better days to come.
I cannot forget
I curse my inability to change things
And despise myself for running away
But I had my own selfish reasons
And futures other than my own to consider
I haven't lost my way
I've just mislaid the map
Perhaps someday too I will return
For nothing else other than to walk the streets of my hometown
But this is one of the greatest burdens the human heart carries
As every exile knows.

In the mists of the Victoria Falls

Where the ferocious and powerful Zambezi pushes its way down
a sheer drop,
over the rock face and through the ravine
I have stood and gazed many a time at the power and magnitude
of the rapids.
I see myself now
At different ages and with different aspects
First as babe getting soaked in my mother's arms
And as a little girl holding daddy's hand
tight lest I slip and fall down Devil's Cataract,
a ten year old running through the forest
with friends at my heels trying beat the rain dripping off the
vegetable ivory palms as rainbows form all around us,
Then with sketch pad and water colours as an artistic and
introspective teenager
Something to show the art teacher
After the holidays.
Finally as an adult
Pondering my life and my family's
Who spent their years on both sides of the bridge
My grandfather, my dad and uncles
Who earned their living on the mines of copper
My older brother and cousins who were born in the north
And the younger ones like me
Who took their national identity from the south
The roar of the water, the spray running off my face
The steamy heat of the twining forest vines
The train thundering down the
tracks cutting a dash on the bridge

Puffing out steam and coughing up black smoke.
The bridge, itself, with its spines and fingers of steel reaching across
the gaping gorge
And the foot passengers, who walked the distance between
Zimbabwe and Zambia
calculating the difference between a mile, one foot in the south
and one in the north.
The arguments about which side had the better views of the Falls,
better fish, colder beer.
All the dusty paths lead to Livingstone,
the eternal guardian of the waters
Glaring down at travellers and tribesmen alike.
A man, explorer, missionary, forever cast in immovable bronze
and how as children, we were filled with wonder at this intrepid
and commanding visionary
Who beat a path where there was none
And forged forward with the Book of the Lord as his only passport.
A man made of myths and legends.
I used to go looking for him on my own.
He seemed such a solitary figure.
I liked being out there in the bush.
As I wondered what his thoughts might have been.
I concerned myself with much more trivial matters,
The monkeys and baboons
scampering in and out of our camp
With their stolen stash from our breakfast table at the *rondavels*
The mozzie nets over our beds
And the stifling heat, so oppressive in the night we could nearly
touch it.
So hot it chased any thoughts of sleep away
My sister and Morag telling ghost stories to while away the hours

between midnight and dawn,
Too awake and too frightened to go to the campsite toilets on my
own.
Lazy afternoons, drowsy in a deck chair
While Dad wrestled with his prize tiger fish
Mum pickling it afterwards
And the sandwiches we all enjoyed.
My sister and I singing "I can't keep it in"
But not wanting to use the drop-hole toilets
Morag keeping cavey in case the boys came sneaking up on us.
The green swimming pool at Dete
All to ourselves.
While Cat Stevens and Elton blared from the supersonic transistor.
The four of us squashed into the back of the old pickup truck
My brother, Mike the leader of the pack
Before he was drafted into the army
he was my hero then and now
But back then I thought he'd always be there to protect me
And he has been ever since.
Then the perilously journey back
Rubber baking on the tarmac
Arriving back in Bulawayo by the mercy of God
After four blowouts between the pickup and the trailer on the
strip roads
And the long wait in the dark bushveld while dad changed the tyres.
Phew!! The witch doctor was right after all
I would live a long and happy life!
I look back at the old family photographs
And I feel happy.
They take me back to that place
Where we lived, and loved and belonged.

Townsend High School, Bulawayo

In the corners of my mind there dwells a place,
A place where I laid my life plan
Formed the ideas that shaped my way of thinking
Where sunlight guided my way through the dark recesses
And surged me ever forward towards enlightenment.
The pathway to my destiny lay in those corridors
Just waiting for the passage of the years to pass.
How I came to find myself a child with dreams and unformed plans
Running to the lessons I loved
Sauntering to the one's I didn't
And simply disappearing in the crowds of girls in their striped frocks
that come and went,
Avoiding the ever-watchful prefects
On the lookout for some uniform misdemeanour,
And the moments of sheer desperation on that first day
When I looked in bewilderment at the time table, the huge hall
and the massive crowd of form ones
Wondering how I would make my mark.
Not understanding where I needed to be.
Drowning in confusion,
a very tiny guppy
in a huge sea of green
Learning the lay of the land
Trying to understand the hierarchy where we were not even
considered to be worthy of a smile from the second formers.
Eyes out on storks reading the graffiti on the walls of the toilets.
The scribbled notes passed from girl to girl until the hawk-eyed
mistress discovered our subterfuge.
The gym teachers who wouldn't take the excuse notes

With forged mothers' signatures
Exercise is essential for your well-being and having a period is
no excuse.
Somehow leaping over hurdles in the 37 degree midday sun held
little attraction for me
As I slunk off to the debating club, crochet club, first aid club, art club
Any club that got me out of sport.
To be in the cool of the library was my heart's desire.
Working among the shelves of my favourite writers
Daphne Du Maurier, Agatha Christie, Doris Lessing who took me
to another world
Beyond my southern African parameters.
Hidden Cornish estuaries, the Torquay Riviera
Murder, mystery and forbidden romance.
And picking up a book from a random selection and reading a
random paragraph
Picked me up and transported me there.
Stories I slipped into with ease and became the unseen onlooker.
And on returning to the classroom,
imagining being right there
At the storming of the Bastille.
To be a part of the Napoleonic army.
Carrying the flag for France.
Liberté, Egalitaré, Fraternité!
Those magnificent educators breathed life into everything.
How I loved them,
Soaked in every word.
And to the others who made little impression on my creative mind
I hope they will forgive me,
the dullness of a tedious afternoon learning Afrikaans
grammatical clauses

Sleepy, brain worn and battle weary waiting for the bell to ring.
Holding my head up with a hand, stray hair, sweat plastered to my
forehead.
Maths algebra, tan, sine and co sine
Trigonometry and Pythagoras theorem
Lordy, Lordy!
Did anyone ever find out who X was?
How they tortured us!!
Day after day, hour after hour
with theories, formulas and equations
when the day seemed so much longer
Than the six periods between Assembly and home time.
Oh youthful summer of our lives,
Promising all that life had to offer
When the world was just a footstep away!
I salute you!
I swear my spirit will haunt those hallowed spaces when I'm gone,
hand in hand
With the ghosts of other girls past.
And when I think of Townsend Girls High
I know a little of my younger self resides there still in the bricks
and mortar
In the echoes of the past
In the shadows of the English stockroom
Where the old books we once held gather dust.
Where is that shy, spotty twelve year old who entered that place
emerging a confident woman
Six years into the future
With principles, loyalties and ideals of her own?
Does she ever think of the old place?
Yes, in her dreams she is there

For our school gave her everything,
Rum flavoured sweets, To Sir With Love, The French Revolution,
lifelong friends and mentors who she hears to this day
Their voices still in live in her head.
Flame lily may you burn forever brightly
And the young ladies who were fortunate enough to wear your
badge
Just above their hearts
May they keep it there ever more.

A little bottle of soil

I collected this at the foot of the *kopje*
On the day we went looking for World's View
I of course had been before
But for the children it was a new adventure
As we played the part of explorers
This was his place, my place
My childhood playground
As I leapt from rock to rock
Ochre, yellow and gold
In those days when I had nothing to do but pass time
And as the years fell away from my eyes
I saw a younger me in my son
The boy climbing and playing with his cousins
And how they hop scotched on the flat surfaces
Like I had done
And picked up pebbles
Discarding the dull ones and pocketing the special,
Treasure for the window ledge
And the little girl
Who pulled at my sleeve
Aunty, can you hear the spirits talking?
The wind rustled through the leaves,
It was so still
It was eerie
I shivered in spite of the sunshine
a sensitive child, this relative of mine
Saw things the others didn't
I sensed them too
Yes, Darling

The place is sacred
The valley of the spirits
Our world and theirs
We were trespassing
We took our photos
Paid our respects and moved on.
But I wanted to take something with me.
I bent down to scrape up the dust
Put it into a bottle
Just fragments of granite
Ground into little grains
Like the family who once climbed up to the top,
We are scattered,
The bottle sits on my bookshelf
A world away, in my Devonshire flat
It is all I have of Africa now,
My tiny piece of the Matopos
Where I spent my childhood
Getting lost on the dusty paths that led me home
And I remember dad's immortal words
"Pack the Landy we're going to the bush."
Mom, Nippy, the terrier, and me
As we shut up the house and dived into the long yellow grass.
Now the wind the blows through the trees
Where the old graves lie undisturbed
And remind us that the children are gone.
Not just me,
Not just mine
But all of them.

The old house on Matopos Road

What happens when we leave a place?
I mean when we physically walk out the door
And remove ourselves from the space.
When the mirror no longer captures
A reflection of our face?
When the house is just an cavernous shell
As the dust particles start to fall from the ceiling
Will something of bespeak of our ever being there
The places we call home,
When our voices are no longer heard echoing in the empty rooms?
I saw a picture of the old house as it is now
The flamboyant tree where I cycled in an endless loop as a child
is now a dry stump
And I wanted to cry for the loss of it.
How the red blossoms painted my world
In days gone by,
The jacaranda tree with dad's engines
Hanging from the branches is gone too
His garage is there but he is not.
The tumbled down stones of my mother's rockery
Where, in the madness of one hot summer,
I made a pool
Damming up the drainage with mud
And paddled with my dog,
And the barrenness of the sparse and arid yard that was once my
tropical paradise
Left my heart sore
It's not how I remember it at all
Hiding in the beautiful gerberas camera shy

Playing forts in the purple paper flowers of the petua bush.
Putting on plays with neighbourhood pals
in the shade of the pine trees.
Tip-toeing to see if my brother was awake
When he returned from his stints in the army
in his cottage bedroom quietly tucked away from the main house.
And how I escaped
Hiding under the verdant cool vegetation
when Mother was on a rampage.
Lifting the lid on dad's worm bath
Throwing in the potato skins
And where we buried our dog
I'll never forget the screech of the breaks
Dad running out,
Carrying Bully's lifeless body.
And how we cried learning the first lesson of loss.
Mom playing the piano
Singing along to chirpy, chirpy cheep, cheep
And beloved Rosen who patched up my cuts and gave me my *sadza*.
That's what I see when I remember that house
My parents loving and fighting and keeping it all together
My brother coming and going
My mother's desperate prayers for his safety
And how our lives changed when he received his call up papers.
Handstands on the grass
Counting the army trucks that passed the gate
Biltong hanging up to dry
These are my memories
Not the picture I see today.
Where did they go, all those years
When Famona was mine?

When the house held us safe from the troubles outside the city's perimeters?
The house still stands in its little corner on the Matopos Road
New families have come after us
Added their presence and no doubt moved on
But for us, it will always hold a piece of my history
A piece of me.

Dare we hope

Should we pray?
Today is the beginning of a new day
In the land where we were born
Could this be the start of a new dawn?
As people arise and take to the streets
Those who can only vote with their feet
Their eyes, their hearts
Could this be our new start?
I will be with them in spirit and voice
There really isn't much of a choice
For we have been scattered too far away
And so overseas is where all exiles stay
And as we look, glued to our screens
At the surreal scene
We cling to a small shred of hope
And pray for blue skies
And that the militia are kind
So put away your guns today
And join hands
Across our land
For peace is coming
Wounds are healing
And with a happy and joyful heart
Look up to the heavens and say
Please Lord, let it be today.

There'll be parties in the old country tonight

The sound of jubilation will echo through the tree-lined avenues
of our home towns
Joyous cheering,
Exuberant dancing
An all-night *pungwe*
As festivities comes early,
People will gather round rural fires
And remember this day
When with one strike of the pen
He was gone,
Resigned, impeached.
Life presidency slipping over the hills
With the setting sun
All our brothers and sisters,
will be smiling
Some even crying
And happiness will spill over
As the car horns fill the streets
With noise and laughter and hope
The king has been toppled off his throne
And no more will his tyranny
Torment the people
No longer will his dynasty pillage our land.
His lineage will not wear the crown
The flag has been reclaimed
In the name of freedom!
The reign of Africa's Hitler is finally at an end.
And in the fading light

We gather from across the globe
To light candles
Raise the glasses
And focus all our attention
on the new dawn to come
Emotions running high
As we remember those who have gone,
The nameless faces who didn't live to tell the tale.
Turn the page, children
this lesson in history is done
No more will his name be hailed
No more will we hear the vitriolic rhetoric
Spewing from his mouth
The people have spoken
The spell is broken
This is our beginning
The journey will not be easy
But step by step
Brick by brick
We will endeavour to be better
This sad story never to repeat
But let's enjoy tonight
Tomorrow we begin the fight
So onward we go together
In love, in unity, in peace forever.

Sound the gong

He is gone!
The time has come
Beat the drum,
Bang the shield
Time to yield,
Not a tear will we shed
For the man who soaked the flag in red
On his hands the blood he bled
Once green –
our fair and beautiful land
Fertile and abundant,
Yellow –
Now turned to sand.
Black is the past
That lies between the red
Like the lies that have been fed
to the people instead of food,
From evil can come no good
And the liberator, turned to tyrant in the blink of an eye
While all we can do is ask why?
Gold is the colour of the bird
Spent on nothing but trinkets
for the self-appointed queen
Shoes, designer clothes, holidays in the east
For the nepotistic dynasty,
While the people suffer
hungry and lean
Watching it all unfold
Helpless to do a thing.

These events were foretold
By sages far wiser
than mere mortals,
Who could see into the future.
Red is the corrupted Marxist star
Fading in the sky.
Excessive greed
While the crocodiles feed
And the house that tumbles into stones.
White are the bones
Hidden in the earth of a mass grave
And no prayers could save.
Shame on you for what you've done,
And as for mercy
I'll show you none
The day of reckoning has come
For as you live so shall you die
And you shall reap what you sow
So do not tarry but please just go.
Sound the gong
He is gone
The man who stayed too long.

In quieter moments

When you find me in deep contemplation
 I am thinking of home
Willing myself back to a time
When it was the only place I knew
All I felt came to me in those early days
Seeped into my soul
Became part of my essential essence
And it is these memories that I try to keep alive
They help me to survive
To navigate this new strange world,
A world where I am a stranger, a visitor
For I can only be a tourist in my own land now.
When you become an exile
Through circumstance, or choice
Sometimes you never go back
And sometimes only for the briefest of moments
You may fly over your home air space
Or be lucky enough to walk there once more,
For true love travels great distances
And she was after all your first love
But you are only a passenger in time
You have arrived at a future date,
Little imagining that you would ever be anywhere else
But those who were once there
Are gone
Either committed to the dust
Or in a foreign soil
Although the walls of your childhood home
embrace you

And in your mind's eye you see your former self

It is only if you listen carefully

That you hear the voices of the past; your parents, grandparents, siblings and friends.

And so my dear kindred spirits

Is it not a kinder thing just to stay away

Before emotion and loss pull you under the tide with grief and longing?

Or is it necessary to answer that call

To your heart, to your soul?

What is this magnetic force

That pulls you south, east and west?

The star that guides you home once more

It is the rhythm of your heart!

So follow it back

Or remain forever severed

This binding bleeding

Dripping, beating, pulsating

Stemless flow

It will not be ignored

For it will never leave you.

We left before the jacaranda season

Before the first rains of summer
When the chill lay on the ground
Before the petunia baskets started to break into bloom at the
Harare Show.
When the dust was dry upon the veld
And before the warm southern breeze started to heave its breath
over the land.
And my heart broke as the plane took off from the runway
And the sobs in my chest could not be stilled
As I looked out of tear-washed eyes for a last glimpse of my
beloved birth place,
And I turned away and cursed the day
I flew away
A heavy hold took grip of my heart
And there it remained.
She is gone, this African child of ours,
We have lost her to the steel grey Northern skies.
And my spirit longed for my place,
The place I belonged
And the home I that I had left
And the vacant space that I once occupied stayed when I was gone.
Now I stand beside a different flag
And have learnt new songs
But look into my eyes and see what I have seen,
Cut open my heart
There it resides
In a little corner
It is with me.
It's is me!

You will see it
My southern African soul.
She comes in dreams
Taps me on the shoulder
And wraps me in her warmth.
And when I think I am alone
she whispers to me.
"Don't worry child, although you have wandered a little too far
You are not beyond my reach.
You belong to me as I belong to you
Because you were given to me
when you were born.
And through my sadness, my loneliness, my alienation
I am content, broken yet whole
It is my strength
It is my truth
"*Thula*, my child," she says "*Lala* now.
I am with you still and always will be."
And she lulls me to my slumber
And I dream I am there still.

Where the flame lilies grow

I sat out among the frangipani and the poinsettia
Breathing in the resplendent morning air.
It had rained in the night
And the Earth had opened its mouth
to receive life-giving moisture,
And I shivered in the coolness of the dawn
As I walked across the lawn and sat under gazebo of vines
The old lab following me and licking the dew from my toes
My head still muzzy from sleep
Blinking as the brilliant white sunlight
Filtered through the palm fronds.
I looked about me,
All the trees I had planted
And those that had loved the garden before me
Little realising that some other hand would
Pick the fruit they had planned to harvest
And I wondered who would take my place
When I was gone
And it struck me that life would go on
in this hallowed corner
The weaver birds would still go about their nest-making
And the jasmine would still fill the air with sweetness,
Even when I was ten thousand miles away,
the flame lilies would still grow and twine about themselves
while I was waking to a cold and dull Christmas morning.
This little scene will be someone else's joy
And my happy hours of labour in this garden would be another
person's reward.
And I hoped someone would taste the juice

of the yellow cling peaches
And not let them fall and lay in waste on the ground for the worms to enjoy.
And I prayed someone would pick my roses and agapanthus
And put them in a vase in the living room,
And have the mango and pawpaw for breakfast on a summer's morn
And gin with a slice of lemon or lime from my trees
When the sun was about to set.
And I remembered the day we bought the house,
And my plans to fill the garden with flowers and fruit in my little patch
And as I sat and pondered,
it occurred to me that we must always plant fruit
And sow the seeds of flowers we love
Even if it becomes another's bounty
For the trees are life and our spirits abide among the blooms
Even when we are gone.
It is primeval
It is part of us, to leave a print of ourselves
in the corners we inhabit
For although they who once passed time here are not here
They have left something behind
And in the silence we hear them,
In the vacant space, we feel them
And perhaps when I am no longer here
and the red veranda where I loved to pass my afternoons may lie empty
Suspended, as in a deep and forgotten sleep
When my absence is all that is felt.
But wouldn't I be so much happier if
Some other hand swept here

and polished away my foot steps in the dust?
And I hope the swinging bench will not lie still on its hinges.
If I'm to be remembered at all,
I hope it's in the laugh of little children
Who will play here
And that the cracks in the wall will be painted over by vivid flowers
of bougainvillea
that someone else will plant,
And so when I think of this place
I won't feel melancholy with images of it going to seed
But I will rejoice that I was fortunate to have been here
and be content to think
Others will cherish it
To start the cycle again
Planting, tending, harvesting
in this place I have loved so well.

It came to me in a dream last night

Cold and dark was the air around
As I slipped into the land of *lala*
And all at once I was transported back,
The sun filtering in through the car windows
African rhythms pouring like sweet oil into my ears
Driving deep into the game park
The road undulating, carrying me along as giddy as a child on a
swing made from an old tyre,
And the Matopo Hills wrapped themselves around me
In the warm embrace so well remembered from the days of my
youth
And as I travelled on I pass crude huts of mud and straw
Village children ran forth to open the gates
keeping the livestock in
And the wild animals out,
Asking for sweets and fizzy cola
The dust on their feet from a decade of dry summers
And their smiles drawing me in and warm eyes that spoke of a
life of simple pleasures.
The cars they had fashioned out of wire,
Necklaces of lucky beans
And stories passed down from the elders.
My heart was filled with their laughter
As my troubles sailed away like a dandelion on the wish of a
child.
The car shaking over the grinding cattle grids
Stirring up clouds of ochre sand in its wake
And the acacia trees showering their blossoms in a curtain of
yellow confetti.

And as I entered into this still and perfect world
I was overcome with a feeling of tremendous peace
Leaving the car under a tree I ventured down a dry path
The earth wrinkled with cracks desperately seeking the gentle rain
to slake its thirst
And quite unexpectedly I came upon
a herd of impala
Unaware of my presence, they continued to graze
The softness in their eyes photographed a gentle image in my
mind's eye
And up above, something caused a dark shadow to flash upon the
ground
As a majestic eagle flew to a higher vantage in among the *kopjes*
I placed myself on a rock,
Imagining my dad sitting patiently fishing beside the dam
And mother making toasted sandwiches in the jaffles on the fire.
When nothing would keep me and Charlie, the labrador, out of
the water.
Those three companions are gone now.
But in the midst of my dream I am here with
the birds, the long golden grass, the trees and the rock rabbit
families scuttling around, in and about the crevices and caves
Black beaded inquisitive eyes
Curious to know why I'm there.
And as I look to the sky I see the sentries of granite held aloft by
some unseen hand
Symbolic of the balance of life
They have been guarding this scene for me
in my absence
And will continue to do so when I have been returned to ashes and
dust.

And I weep
for I have returned to my true north
Ironically in a southern corner of the world.
And reaching down I kick off my shoes
Earthing myself to the land as in my barefoot days of childhood,
Feeling the magnetic energy spreading through my core
As I soak up the sun's warmth and it's blinding light.
And capture this moment to remember for the future
Just letting the solitude of this sacred spot
Seep once more into my soul.
When I awake from the dream
There is a lightness to my spirit
As I open my eyes to face the day.
The darkness engulfs me
shivering in the stark coldness of a January morning.
Reaching out to turn on the radio
I catch the last of the weather report
"Mostly cloudy with a chance of rain – maximum temperature,
minus two"
But it does not bother me this morning
For I have returned from a journey to my spiritual home.

A long time ago

A long time ago when the world was quite small
And we felt safe
And we explored it on our bicycles
And went miles and miles
And the grownups didn't know where we were,
And little did they care
As long as we were indoors by the time the street lights came on
And we took off early in the morning
And bought crisps for five cents
And an orange ice lolly for three cents
And we pilfered our parents spare change
And spent our ill-gotten gains
On marshmallow fish and apricot sweets
And pretended the sweet cigarettes were real
And we could blow smoke rings like our big brothers
And all Mum and Dad's friends were our aunties and uncles
And our real aunties and uncles were like our parents
And could clout us across the ear
If we stepped out of line.
And we were looked after by the maids and gardeners who loved us
just because they did,
And spanked us across the legs if we were naughty
And we went to the bioscope on Saturday night
And to church every Sunday
And we sneaked out of the house
When the parents were snuggly tucked up for the night
To steal cokes in the industrial sites
And swim in other people's pools
And we knew all the neighbourhood dogs by name

And they knew us and would never give us away
And we spied on our big sisters and their boyfriends
And saw them sunbathing and smooching
And we laughed when they used vinegar and oil for sun tan lotion.
And we went to Durban on holiday
And bought Fredos and Penny Cools at the tuck shop
And life was okay, *ek sê*
And everything was *lekker*
And we had water fights with the hose pipe
And built forts in the back garden
And only got toys at Christmas time
And nobody entertained us but ourselves.
And we played on swings made from old tyres
And the teacher was boss
And the headmistress was queen
And heaven help us if they ever had to phone our parents.
And we felt secure and loved and disciplined
And we knew where we stood in the food chain
And we were happy with that
And we never questioned our parents authority
We wouldn't dare!
Under a southern sun
Was where it all began
Where we grew, and we learned
and we were loved by all
A long time ago when the world was quite small.

Once upon a time a girl from Africa

Once upon a time a girl from Africa
Moved into a flat in England,
All alone and dealing with many issues,
She sat on the carpet
At her lowest ebb
And started to cry.
There was so much she wanted to say,
So much she wanted to get out of her system,
She was homesick
She was lost
She was missing everybody she loved,
Her bones were cold
She was tired of grey sky clouds,
She missed the sunshine
And the warm smiles of Africa,
She missed the girls she taught at the Convent.
Now she could have reached for the gin,
She could have reached for the tablets
But instead she reached for pen and paper
And started to write things down
And it started to seep out of every pore
She dug very deep
To get to the heart of the pain,
And all the memories
Good and not so great
Started coming
And she found that she could write down anything,
She could talk about anyone,
So she did

Her muses were discussed and disguised in her lines,
And at first her family and close friends
Liked her writing and said kind things
But as time went on
More people started to read her work
And share thoughts and ideas,
And suddenly our poet discovered she wasn't lonely anymore
Because other people felt the same way
About a lot of things
And all she needed to do was just to reach out
And hold other hands
And connect to that great big family in the universe,
Because that's what we all need,
to know that there are others
That need us as much as we need them.
Poetry has been her therapy
And she was grateful for this gift
she discovered she had.
And for the greater gift of being able to share it.
Thank you for all the support and love
And for your friendship
And for all the stories we share.
At the end of the day
That's all we need,
Some to care.

The house in Greendale

If I think about it now and remember the house
Where our boys grew up
I see a different place to you,
I loved the long drive
The expansive garden
The avocado trees
It was a place I escaped
A place I changed
A garden I grew
Where we held birthday parties for Tim
And children came
And cakes were baked,
And Doug arrived from the bush
Unannounced to find me cooking in the nude by the stove,
I'd look up and my nephew would be there
Weary and worn from his animal conservation out of town
A quick dash to throw on a gown
And let him in.
It was a place we filled with animals
Three dogs, Jacquie, the doleful labrador and
Nipper and Jock
The terrible terriers
Where our daughter was conceived
And her first home
Where the boys and I bought
Fresh fruit every day from Honey Dew farm and made
fruit salads for lunch
Green vegetables from the women on the corner
To feed the rabbits, that multiplied in great number

Where our friends and families gathered under the trees for
our wedding
At the end of one warm August
Our first wedding dance
Neil Diamond,
Baskets of petunias
Pots of red anthuriums
Agapanthus and red hot pokers
Macadamia nuts,
Pecans that fell from the trees,
Where Tim started school
New kittens
And tortoises running off into the compost heap.
I don't see it like you,
The house of terror
The place where a little boy cried outside to get away from the
fights within.
The nights, the demands written on the calendar,
To me it was a place of hope
A sanctuary of escape after the grotty flats in the avenues,
Where we stretched our legs,
Where my boy learned how to ride a bike
And yours to read,
Where I held a daughter to my heart,
And the champagne
Cliff and Jane arrived with
When we brought her home.
The house has memories
But not the sort you house.
I speak of it fondly
For although it was full of ups and downs

It was also a house where I learned endurance
And patience,
To put on a happy face,
Even through many weathers
There is always light and dark
In any space
I am at peace with that place.

Falling blossoms of the jacaranda tree

We are the falling blossoms of the jacaranda
Where, in the unscathed days of our childhood
We played, and danced in violet raindrops.
To awaken in the morning and view an outstretched avenue
Carpeted and canopied in purple
As far as the eye could see,
Brought a quiet calm to the soul.
The solitude of a summer's afternoon
Paintbrush in hand,
With nothing but a desire to capture
The beauty of the splendid haze
As I blotched water and paint onto a pad,
Is a memory I hold in that locked drawer in my mind,
With keys that are hidden
And only I can find.
And the first flourish of love
And how we walked through a grove of trees
Hand in hand,
Feeling the coolness of the air
After the rain had taken the lid off the heat,
He liked to wear purple,
This man of mine,
Told me it was the colour of kings
Majestic, regal, enduring, everlasting,
And so we were thus
A proud family of beings
Growing and loving among the trees
That lined every city
And every town

In a place we called our own
In the days when we believed
This kingdom was ours to keep.
And then came the turmoil
And that shook the boughs
And even though we tried to cling on,
All hope was gone
And so we fell one by one
From the branches of that strong dark trunk
Some of us were crushed,
Most blown away,
For blossoms are not meant to stay.
And now they stand in a solitary line
For they are waiting for a time,
And every summer they put on a magnificent show
In their row upon row
For they are hoping that one day
The children of the purple cloaks
Will return
They have gone away
That lesson to learn.
Because you see
It is what it will always be
That the heart will lead you home.

The story of a crocodile

Somewhere in the middle of southern, central Africa a tired and frustrated people wait for change. They are hopeful and yet cynical, for can there ever be change while things remain the same?

I will tell you a story of a crocodile...
In the green phosphorus depths of the river
The crocodile lays in wait.
Slow and calculated are his movements,
Stealth, his weapon
Deceptive camouflage conceals his evil intentions,
To the animals peacefully drinking on the bank
he is a floating log
But what lies beneath is dark and horrible;
Slimy green reptilian eyes
Move closer
Waiting for the opportune moment to pounce
And he has waited a long, long time for this,
Felt the hunger in his belly
Been a stooge and bystander
Played the part of one alongside,
Propped up the regime
Hoping for the old hyena and his bitch to pass
Became the regime,
A stalwart
A mechanism in the abuse of power,
And akin to his very nature
He has crept up from behind
Staged a coup

Giving the people a chance to hope,
But it was a masquerade
A well-produced act in a play
And the hyenas are alive and well
Growing fat in their dotage
While the people starve,
And the crocodile is now the forerunner in the race.
He is not the saviour
He will not bring salvation
Can a lion lie down with the lamb?
He is a crocodile
His only intention is death
He has instilled fear into your hearts
Never forget it!
His hands are stained with blood
As are those of his ilk
His brothers in arms.
Remember the company he keeps
He cannot hide behind a smile and good intent,
Do not be made the subject of a joke,
You have suffered too long.
Two generations have gone by.
A crocodile is a crocodile,
Prehistoric
An ancient, cunning beast,
If you saw him sleeping in the sun
You could poke a stick at him and believe him to be harmless
But look at his open mouth as he dozes,
Look at his teeth
Look at his immense bulk
He will crush you with one swipe

Drag you under to your very death
In his watery lair
Don't go too close
Do not be fooled my brothers and sisters by his crocodile tears
For even while he sleeps
His eye is open
He watches all
He his waiting
He will not change
He has survived for a reason,
For a purpose.

A piece of clay

If I were to take a piece of clay
And mould a child
How she would be made?
From the blood of her kith and kin
running in her veins
And the ancestors would know the child's name
Before she was born
This child of the African soil,
Child of the burning sun
And they would be waiting
For her to fulfil her destiny
And walk beside her every step of the way
The child would be comforted, feeling them close
Protecting her from harm
Great grandmother's eyes would become her own
And her course would be set by southern stars
Swathed in midnight blue by night,
And azure skies by day
And the sun would give warmth to her shoulders
Like a golden blanket,
Like her brother who has walked the path before her,
Our children would never be alone
Because the ancestors would guide them
And behind the softness of their lashes
A million images would be imprinted
In their brains
The smell of the rain
The open wet earth
The rock rabbits leaping through the balancing rocks

A blazing red sunset
And they would listen to tales of old
Beside the camp fire light
And awaken to the softness of a new dawn through the acacia trees
And they will write their names with sticks in the dust
As they are written in the book of life,
In family Bibles,
And their forebears would smile
Because they would recognise themselves in a mother's sister name
Or a father's brother,
And the child would carry their lineage like a cloak upon
their backs
And their stories would live in their minds from tales half heard
While they were sleeping on their mother's bosom,
And the journeys they travel will be shared by those seen and unseen,
As they try to unravel the mystery of it all
A voyage of an ancestor across the sea from lands of green and mist
Many years ago
To the land of sun, bush-veld and new opportunities
New nationalities, new mother tongues
And our grandsons will share the names of our brothers, our father
and our great grandfathers
And so through us they live again.
For we are who we are
The more we change, the more we cling to our heritage and our past
And so we remain the same.
And for this reason we are born
and reborn again.

In a country nestled between two rivers

Is where I was born
A rich and abundant place
I was surrounded by a beautiful people
Who spoke a melodic language
Clicks rolled off their tongues
And flowed into my infant ears,
They carried the sunshine in with their smiles and aromatic smells
of woodsmoke on their clothes,
I felt the earth through my bare feet
Magnetised to the land,
Played with toy cars the village children made out of wire
And we wished on lucky bean necklaces
As the Kalahari breathed its hot breath
Over us in Matabeleland
And in the distant haze
You could see a mirage coming off the road
And underfoot, the melting tarmac
Gooey
Burning our soles in thin sandals and *tackies*
Rainfall was gift from the heavens
And we gave thanks for it
Danced and laughed because the gods had been kind,
It meant life
It meant crops
It meant the farmers could survive another season of bank loans
The animals could slake their thirst at waterholes.
We scooped watermelon out with our bare hands
And ate our fill
And drank juice out of its shell,

Because we remembered the dry seasons
When no rain came
And rivers dried up
And water was rationed
And we shared the bath water,
Grateful even though it was dirty
Then we used it to flush the loo.
It was a precarious balance
Between life and death
When it was good it was paradise
And when it was bad we carried on
Made a plan,
And when we left
We left our hearts and our childhoods there
Memories and everything we once were.
Nobody understands who we were,
What we achieved in our lives in the land forgotten by time and
turmoil,
Everything we once had
Slipped like sand through the fingers in our hands
And there was nothing we could do it prevent it.
I recently saw a photograph of a friend
In his youth
Posted on social media
He had been a South African
rock star in another life
Someone famous.
And it made me realise we have all made journeys
Traversed the miles
Left our histories behind.
Came over as clean slates

Having to prove ourselves.
I keep warm remembering
Life as a child,
Starting school,
a Bulawayo Convent girl in blue checks
Little ponytails,
And going full circle to become a teacher,
An educator of young ladies,
We read Wordsworth, Shakespeare and Dylan.
Things Fall Apart, The Lion and the Jewel.
We skipped through the daffodils
And marvelled at Stonehenge and
Hampton Castle from the windows
of the Harare Convent
Keen to believe things were better beyond the walls that kept us safe.
My girls were intelligent, eager to learn
And in another time,
Would have taken their place in a strong and vibrant society
But they were keeping things together
While their parents were out of the country,
Earning pounds to stave off the poverty at home.
Chido, Thembi, Catherine, Katie, Aisha, Rudo,
Where are you all now?
I hope you achieved your dreams,
Your teacher has seen these places,
And yes they are magnificent
But not how we imagined
When we were creating our own adventures,
Now I sit in the flat
Surrounded by books
My own form of escape,

Loneliness has its own compensations
At least I'm left alone
To wallow and dream
And to remember a time
When I was respected
Held in high regard
And considered a trail blazer.
And these things remind me
of our former lives
Of our glorious past.

There's something about eating a mango

That always reminds me of home
Maybe it's the colour
That sends me straight back
To sitting on the back step
In the blazing sun
Picking the mango strings from my teeth
The fruit all squishiness in my hands
And the sticky juice on my chin
Rosen scolding me for ruining
A perfectly clean white t-shirt
And knowing she would later scrub her fingers raw to remove
the stain;
Or perhaps it's the way they make me feel
All golden, replete and happy,
After I've indulged all my senses,
Remembering a time when I'd be
Curled up in the shade of the avocado pear tree,
Not a scrap of it left except the pip.
Perhaps it's the women I recall
With their enamel bowls in the makeshift market
Outside the Bulawayo town Hall
Calling one dollar for five
Their baskets perfectly balanced
On their white starched *doek*-clad heads
Chubby babies tied with Merlin towels
To their backs
In those golden years of childhood.
The mango tree after the rain
Droplets falling off the spear-shaped leaves

The joy of growing my own
Later in life.
The taste, as the flavour hits my palate
And the scent that travels to the back of my throat and into my nose
If I close my eyes while I'm savouring it
I can almost imagine
I am in the land where it was grown
In the land where I was grown
And suddenly from all the fibre of my being
I am back home.

My life is like an upside-down snow globe

Day after day I sit by this window
Watching the sky
As it changes from blue to grey
Grey to white
The grey makes me blue,
Even so the light is spectacular
in the northern hemisphere
I am drawn to it even when there are clouds.
I recall a time when our art teacher
In a fit of excitement
Would send us to a window
To paint the greyness in the sky
You didn't see it often in Zimbabwe
Not for long at any rate.
I am happier looking at the sun
Had I known it at the time
I would have insisted on painting a patch of blue
To carry with me at all times,
I'd like a globe with yellow grass
And animals that roam the savannah
The soft eyes of the impala
The camouflage of the giraffe.
I'd shake it and see sunbeams instead of snow,
I really don't like the cold
I cannot function below 16 degrees Celsius
My brain goes into a state of petrification
My body tells me it's time to hibernate.
I'm a tropical flower, you see
My optimum temperature is between 25 and 35

Although I'm getting used to the changing of the seasons
Winter is heavy going
English friends laugh at my layers
I must carry half my weight around in clothes
By 4pm it's dark
My mind tells me it's bedtime!
There is a plaque on my wall
Time stands still there
I call it Bulawayo O'clock
I prefer it
It takes me away from the pressures
The worries
The early mornings,
I look at it and all I see is the elephant
And the words
Si Ye Pambili
"Let us go forward"
And yet I harken back
As if I am frozen in time
Encapsulated in the sun globe
I believe if I can travel back to a warm place
Life would be more bearable,
By nine O'clock at night
I am shivering
And It's time to turn in
Just one more chance to look out the window
On a cloudless, night the stars invite me to linger a bit longer
I can't bear the thought of setting the clock for the morning
When once again I awake in the dark.
Give me the sun
Give me the summer

Give me Bulawayo O'clock
The sun always shines there
At least it does in my mind,
Jumping on a bicycle
And peddling out to the Matopos
Spending a night in the camp at Maleme
And night walking,
And star gazing in an open patch of veld
Stretching my arms wide
Embracing the space
Hugging the universe.
But that was then
And this is now
In the endless space of the long winter's night
I dream a hundred dreams
Flipping through the images
Imprinted in my subconscious mind;
And I pick the paint brush up
To construct something new
And I paint a patch of blue.

Restful respite

I wish I was settling down for an afternoon snooze
In the coolness of a big room with red veranda floors
And large windows thrown open wide,
So wide that I could hear the cicadas
Lulling me off to sleep
With the sun on the candlewick bedspread
Warming my toes
Solid wooden rafters
Lovingly holding up a thatched rooftop
Sturdy dark teak wood furniture
Cream crocheted cloths
Homemade patch-work cushions
Gran's verdant fern spilling out over the top of a copper pot,
The smell of wood fires from the nearby village wafting in mixed
with Jasmine perfume and orange blossom
And pungent khaki *bos*
The burst of colour from the bougainvillea in the near distance
The chatter of women's voices as they pass on the dusty path
And the silence when they've gone
No man's land
The space between consciousness and dreaming
As I give myself over to complete relaxation
And allow my body to heal
My spirit to rest
In a haven of respite
And as I return to this cocoon of safety
Womb-like and familiar
Where the passing from day to night
Is just a trick of the light

With the breathing in of the fresh, resplendent air
I am reborn
Revitalised
At one with it,
The hustle and bustle is finished now
No more will I strive to do more
No more will push myself to brink of exhaustion
The debt is paid
The deed is done
As I surrender into the arms of oblivion.

A rhino's last tears

The last white male rhino laid his head on the ground
Goodbye cruel world was all he could say
And we posted his picture on Facebook
And he even made the main news
And those of us who remembered
The innocent days of our youth
When we saw these beautiful animals roam peacefully
through our savannah world
With whispered warnings from our parents and teachers
To go quietly
Otherwise they would charge,
Heard our hearts cry out
With sadness and desperation
When we heard the news,
As a another fragment of our childhood
Blew away with the newspaper headlines
on the breeze of another pathetic apology from the human race,
And all through the ages, our forebears bore witness to our
terrible plight
As we hurtle towards the edge
Unaware of our own destruction,
As another animal disappears from sight
into the annals of history.
EXTINCTION is a horrible word
Like DEATH
It cannot be reversed
And when the elephants and ostriches have disappeared too
we will return to our plastic world
And our flat screen televisions

And electrostatic energy
Where we are the star of our own soap opera,
And forget when we ran through the long yellow grass
Energised by the sun,
When coming across, quite by chance
A leopard asleep on a rock
Was the most wonderful thing we had ever seen,
Or when we had to wait
For the python that blocked the bush road
From edge to edge
To wend his way across,
And when we teach our children and grandchildren the alphabet
And we get to "R is for Rhinoceros"
And they ask what's that,
We will turn on our tablets and virtual worlds
And show them on YouTube
While we hang our heads in shame.
And to the trophy hunters who shot for fun
Like it was all a great game
I hope you're proud of the glazed dead glass eyes that stare back
at you
How clever we are
To take a beautiful thing,
Murder it and mount it on the wall,
And then congratulate ourselves for our masculine prowess.
To those blessed men and women who made conservation their
lifetime calling,
We thank you,
For you tried to stop the illegal trade of rhino horn and ivory for
eastern market
Medicine and aphrodisiacs

How impotent do we feel now?
And to Sudan, the last of these splendid beasts
The only word I can offer as an epitaph is
SORRY.
And I realise that this doesn't cover it
And doesn't make up for the indiscriminate murder of your
species
But I am very sorry we didn't care enough
From the bottom of my heart,
Apologies from my generation and the ones before me.
We really didn't know what we were doing.

I am a princess

With stars for a diamond tiara
And flowers for my pearl anklets,
My early years were surrounded with blessings,
And the *dwalas* were my uncles,
And the soft round *kopjes* were my aunts,
And when I scrambled up the rocks
Like a *dassie*,
Unseen hands protected me
And stopped me from falling.
I have seen the animals of the veld
The shy little nala,
An impala's soft eyes
And I have heard lions in the night
feeling the paralysing fear,
Sending out desperate pleas to my ancestors to let the soft canvas
of the tent be as strong as a bricked fortress.
I have watched a herd of elephants walk passed our car,
So close we could touch them,
With their matriarchal strength,
As we held a collective breath
In silent respect.
I've heard the hyenas bark in the dark
And listened to fireside tales
Of ghosts and *nangas* who walked these dusty paths,
I've witnessed my dad wrestling with a tiger fish
On the banks of the Zambezi,
And have been completely awestruck by the beauty and majesty
of the Victoria Falls.
I have wandered deep into the Matopos

Seen so many *blouskop* lizards that my heart gave a leap,
I've picked chameleons off grapevines
And rescued them from the road,
And even seen a *legavaan* slip out of the water
Giving me the fright of my life in the dead of night,
I've had bilharzia
And felt the fever of malaria
I have scars all over my limbs from an active African childhood,
My skin finds it's bronze pigment when I'm in the sun
And I have my own unique language
Extracted from a mixture of Sindebele, Shona, Afrikaans and
English,
This image you see of me now
Is not what defines me,
This is a person who has left the precious kingdom
This is a person who carries
A thousand sorrows on their back
And a million images in their mind,
A person who has nothing but their culture to guide them,
It is stamped into my psyche
It goes straight to my core,
I am a person
Learning to live with a new identity,
To fit in with another culture,
Albeit with gratitude and acceptance.
So reserve your judgement
For I have dealt with tremendous change.
Experience has been my teacher,
But it's not who I am.
I am a princess,
Born in the royal seat of Khumalo

Bulawayo,

Rhodesia,

Zimbabwe

This is my land ...

between two mighty rivers ...

Zambezi and Limpopo

And so I must carry myself with dignity,

Though my country be a distant memory to me now,

And my kinsfolk be far,

For we princes and princesses have been banished to the world's
four corners

By a cruel and horrible tyrant

Who thrives on milk and honey

In his dotage,

A pretender to the throne,

While we, the forgotten children,

Of the royal household,

navigate a new territory alone.

Just another day

To the rest of the world
Today is just another day,
So our country made the headlines
And earned a little clip on the main news,
Interest has been piqued,
By the wider international community,
For all of us who had to go
I hope you realise, I hope you know
That we watch, hope and pray
We cannot exercise our right to cast our vote
And this stabs at our hearts,
How we wish we were there,
As each sad year goes by
We feel the pain deeper
We have not left you
Through choice
And the tears we cry for you
Are always just below the surface,
Today we cry again
Today we hope again
Today we watch again
Our thoughts are with you
We stand with you.
We lift you up to the never ending blue sky
And ask for peace, ask for fair play
And ask for transparency
Just this once,
To our brothers and sisters
Who can go to the ballot box

We pray that your vote
Will find its way to right place
And tonight when the counting starts
We pray with all our hearts for freedom.
We pray for a new era
We pray for a new day
We are with you in spirit
Not in borrowed robes
Far away.

Homeland

I thought I was strong
Always believed love would carry me through
Thought I'd always be with you,
Wanted to be there,
I wanted to be the difference
Between right and wrong,
I wanted to be a trailblazer
Right into the heart of you,
Hoped love would heal the wounds,
And with our pens and our minds we could make change happen,
That we would love you,
Protect you,
And save the next generation from the heartache we knew,
In the battles that were fought
There were no victors,
Everyone lost
The one thing they loved -
You!
History may be written by the government of the day,
But it cannot hide the truth
Though it tries to bury the bodies,
We all know are just below the surface,
With the pain that beats in our exiled hearts,
We go through many phases
Put on our masks
Try to start again
With nothing but our values in our back pockets,
Values that are now redundant
In this cold and calculating world,

Where greed will step over your slowly dying body
To get to the next pot of gold,
We pretend we're stronger
We're better off here
And yes we are,
Given the hopeless state of affairs at home,
We have saved our own precious skins
At the expense of the ones we left behind,
We go it on our own
In our own disparate ways,
But that's not who we are
Not what we were
Our family is gone
That great big vibrant family
We once had,
It went when we left you,
We live alone
In a place where no one seems to care
And quietly kill ourselves for the dollar bill
Slowly unravelling at the seams
In the privacy of our sanctuaries
We only see at night,
Where we eat to our full when others are starving at home
We used to share a communal bowl
It nourished us all,
No one sees us picking ourselves up off the carpet
Or the drugs we take to deaden the silence,
Or the tears
The angry frustrations;
We all wanted to stay
To bring our skills to feed your table,

But now we are still waiting for the day
And facing the prospect of growing old
In the cold
No hand to hold in our final hour,
Wasted years,
Emotions that spill over into the drain,
I believed in happy endings
I believed in forever
I hope you understand why I had to board that plane
Because the hardest thing I've ever had to do
Was to walk away from you.

Girl from Gubulawayo

Lapa side where the elephant grass reaches your waist
And a child and her dog can get completely lost
Did I spend my childhood days,
And when I was knee high to a grasshopper
Did I *lala* on the back of my African mother,
And us *picininis* played the days away
Watching the *shongololos* laying on our bellies and caught flying
ants after the rains
And barefooted we left our foot prints in the dust
In the place where we were born
And in the *gumadulas* we ate marulas and wild oranges
And chewed sugar cane and thought it was *lekker*,
Chameleons crawled along our arms,
And dad hung the *biltong* up and we couldn't wait till it was dry
enough to *puza*
And we copied the languages we heard
Khuluma!
And *hey, wena* you knew you were in for it when Mama said *la
gu tshaya*
And someone shouted *gijima*!!
But it was too late
You pushed your luck too far!
And the clip around your head that followed
Eish!! That was a hard *klap*!
Eina man!
But us *abantwanas* learned respect for our elders from an early
age!
Buya lapa, hlalapanzi,
But we were wrapped in love

And everyone knew their place
And just because we were the littlest ones
Didn't mean we were the least important
We were everyone's treasures
Sanibonani nkhosikazi!
And you loved it when you were called a princess
Even though you had mud on your legs
And your dress was torn
And full of blackjacks
And you had run away before they had a chance to brush your hair,
But you ate your doorstep peanut butter sandwiches and sweet tea with condensed milk
And *sadza* and *nyama* for lunch
And heard people shouting greetings across the bush path,
And your parents said you were growing up wild
And you didn't know any different
Because said you wanted to *hlala guhle* when they *hamba* to town
Hey *wena ulamanga!*
Yebo!
Ngiyabonga we are thankful
We will *kholisa* here
Lapa side
Ikhaya.

World's View

The beautiful soft gem squash sun was high
In a bright cornflower blue sky
And stretching out my arms
The vista was vast and my horizon limitless on this glorious day,
The view worth every laborious peddle
From the outskirts of the city
to outreaches of the game park
And here in the remote silence
As I climb up the *gomo*
I feel my spirit ease
My troubles evaporating in the mirage
Over yonder,
The sweet perspiration clinging to my forehead as I head up the
rounded rock face
Mottled with lichen and bleached by the sun
And the *blouskop* lizards consider me from their crevices
And dassies scuttle to hide
A human intruder disturbing their peace
And there amongst the larger boulders
The grave and a slab
The last remains of a man
Who had one foot in the south and one in the north
And saw the birth of an empire
laid the tracks
From the Cape to Cairo
And the people he beguiled along the way
In this place where the spirits wander
Where men met to have a great *indaba*
I can only but wonder

How men are judged by their endeavours
And how hindsight can be a cruel teacher
And like every lesson, we must take the good with the bad,
And how he lies in a tomb of granite
Once a visionary and a renegade
Who brought riches to a far off kingdom
To an overseas queen,
Out here in the bush one can lose sight
Of his achievements
His decisions, his ideas
And now he is castigated for his expansion into the hinterland
I sit and think and consider
How is this any different from the major powers of today?

The smell of the rain

Oh praise the heavens
It has come again,
This precious gift from the skies
Bringing cool respite,
And for all of us who know
What it is to wait through endless days
Not knowing if the gods will smile on us
Or curse the land,
No one praises the rain like an African,
We have seen successive droughts
And felt the harshness of the furnace
All around
With its vice grip
Squeezing lifeblood out of every living thing
We have felt the trepidation
Of yet another year,
Crop failure
Water levels dissipating
Dams evaporating from our very eyes,
Animals dying beside empty waterholes
Rural people eking out survival in the dust
And the relentless thirst,
As farmers look skyward
And say silent prayers.
Life in the balance.
This year we have been blessed
As the sweet rain,
Goddess of life itself
Unites with Mother Earth

And gives birth to abundance once more.
I can only watch from a distance now
But my heart is joyful for my home land
How I wish I was there to dance in the rain with you!

Cosmos by the railway line

My cousin, Bev and I
In the days when we were very young
Decided to *"bly 'n bietjie"*
with her big sister, Di
And so it was to Ogies
We did travel
Taken by car from Johannesburg and left by Aunty Jean for the
week,
Now you've heard the expression I'm sure
One-horse *dorp*
Well, for Ogies in the mid-seventies,
I think if there ever was a horse
It had long since departed,
But Bev and I played the days away with Clair and Bobsy,
Di's little ones
And every day we four would wander
Babies in the prams
Down the dusty road
To the one shop that sold sweets, fizzy drinks and crisps
Pink Panther chocolates, Fanta Grape
and Nik-Naks chips
The place was a dust bowl for sure
Flat for as far as the eye could see
And Ogies hadn't seen much,
Miners that came and went,
You really felt you'd reached the end of the road,
A perfect place to disappear
Under the vastness of the sky
And the tall yellow grass,

But just beyond the shops
Under the fence
Where we'd sometimes stray
Was a profusion,
A wonderful display
Of soft pastel pink
White and mauve
Just beside the railway
Where the cosmos
Ran wild,
And so in this place
Of dry desolation
Bev and I found our salvation
Among the beauty of the blooms.
You couldn't pick them
And put them in a vase
They just wouldn't survive.
Bev is in heaven now
She watches over me every day
Like she did when she was here,
And those memories I often revive,
The precious times we spent together
My bosom cousin-friend
When every year I travelled south in April for my vacation,
And think of those four beautiful children
Who once spent our Easter days behind the petrol station.

Africa calling

Africa pulls at my heart like a magnet
Calls to me while I sleep
In the depths of my despair
She sees me floundering,
Crying out,
I feel like I've lived half my life
With something missing
As I stare out my window
At dismal skies,
And wonder why I'm here,
What would happen if I returned?
Fear keeps me away
At least here I feel safe,
If not content,
There are times when I feel
All of life's joy has left me
And the only thing that keeps me going is my culture,
The knowledge that I know something that they don't,
I have this thing inside me
That burns
And warms the cold longing in my soul,
Like a raging veld fire
And in my loneliness I am whole
If not complete,
Here there is security
But in that land over yonder
Lies my happiness,
How do I bridge the gap
Between yesterday and tomorrow

My former self and now,
What am I waiting for?
What am I living for?
Must I answer the call
Or live and wait to die here
Should I just return
Once and for all ?

A child and his grandfather

A child and his grandfather
sat one day looking out over the escarpment,
"I want to go to London,"
"I have been."
"I want to see the queen."
"She too, I have seen."
"I want to go up high on the London Eye."
"Up here you can touch the sky, watch the eagles as they fly."
"I want to travel the world."
"I have been to many countries of the world."
"Which was the best?"
"This one."
"But the riviera, Italy and Spain, the sea."
"We have the sun and the rain, animals that roam free."
"I want to go on the Tube, ride in a London bus.
What will I be when I grow up?"
"Why what's the rush?
The world will be waiting,"
"What will I be like when I am a man?"
"Older and wiser, and you will remember these days with your
old grandfather.
And when the world has taken everything from you,
and you are part of the rat race,
You will return,
For this is your place,
This is your space."
And reaching up the child took his hand,
He did understand.
"Let's walk, Grandfather."

And so they walked and they talked.
And when many summers had passed
He left him standing there
On that dusty bush path
To find his way
In a land faraway
Where he toiled night and day,
One day he heard grandad
Had passed away
But he continued with his work
Not being one to shirk
He put it behind him
Until the day he thought
About what his grandfather had taught,
And he took his weary body
And headed back
On a plane in the chilly rain
To the land of the sun
To where it had all begun,
And he walked the path out to the escarpment once more
And out there he looked across the plain
And thought of grandfather again
And he realised he had been right
And his soul took flight
For this is where he belonged
And although his grandfather was gone
He heard an eagle cry
Way up high
And at the moment he just knew,
And on the breeze he heard him whisper
"I have always been with you."

Just a dream away

I imagine myself sitting on sun-baked granite rocks
Watching a black eagle circling the sky
In the silence of the day,
Away from my worries
With the *dassies*
And *blouskop* lizards for company,
And if I live to be a hundred years old
My soul will always find its peace there
Among the majesty of the balancing rocks,
Scattered like pebbles
By some giant hand,
Placed to restore the balance
My balance
The epicentre of my quiet calm
My homeland
The Matopos
Where I spent my childhood
My wilderness playground,
Dad fishing
Mom sitting beside him on a deck chair
And I skimming for tadpoles among the reeds,
Cousin Keith, barefoot
Running in the bush looking for game,
These memories tug at my heart
They are the ghosts that haunt me,
The cattle
The dust
Village children opening gates,
Wide eyed with enamel bowls

Waiting for coins and sweets,
My name written in the soil with a stick
Bones thrown
Futures determined
Mine to travel over the seas
Ours dispersed,
And so it was that the children
of Southern Africa
Were severed from all they knew
But we live, we breathe
As one,
With every beat of our Southern African hearts,
Our pointless yearning
The pull towards home
A force we resist every hour of the day
Even though there is nothing for us there,
Our tears could break the harshest drought
And make the dusty ochre earth
Verdant again,
When will the land be healed?
When will we return?
When will our people be united?
When will the scourge be purged?
Why have we been so cruelly cursed
Please let this suffering end
Surely it's time to stop the bleeding?

African

In my reflection on the water
And my image in the mirror
You stare back at me
In my dreams
In my psyche
You are all I see,
The things I have bought
And in my thoughts
The paintings on my wall
In my ornaments, animals
And instruments
Everything and all
Embeds a memory,
A message,
A fragment of you,
In the vibrancy of my clothes
In my language
In my prose
Your map is my talisman
It hangs around my neck
I keep it close to my heart
My beginning
My start
I whisper your name in my prayers
And thank you for the years
You gave me
Nurtured me and the lessons you taught me
I took nothing from you
But wisdom,

That was all I had to keep,
With the tears that I weep
For the longing that will never leave me,
It is my passport
That will one day lead me back,
When my eyes see the tall yellow grass
And the distant blue mountains
Hear the cry of the fish eagle
And stand on the rocky outcrop
Then I will know
I am home.
And I will write my name in the dust,
For this is where one day I must,
Leave my body
Buried in your soil.

Prayer for Zimbabwe

I cannot patch up my breaking heart with any more plasters,
It bleeds for my brothers
It bleeds for my sisters,
It bleeds for the children
Going hungry
It bleeds for the elderly
Cowering terrified
In the dark,
It bleeds for those who need urgent medical attention,
Lifesaving treatment,
But cannot be administered because no one can step out,
Imprisoned in their homes
For fear of their lives,
It cries for families separated
wracked with worry
About their loved ones
People petrified by the unknown and the known dangers,
And all we can do is look on
In helpless frustration,
It finally hit home today,
This is real
This is happening
Please let good prevail
Let the leaders call a halt to this
Let common sense rule the day
Our tears may not save you
Our prayers may not deliver you
But it is all we have to give you,
And please God throw your loving hands over our beloved land

Deliver us from evil
Bring peace
Bring healing
Wash away the hurt
Please bring Zimbabwe out of this storm
Before it is too late.

Oliver

There's a sadness that seeps into the soul
When a good person dies
Knowing that the space will never be filled
And the laughter and the joy
And the music and the melodies he brought
Will be consigned to history
It's even sadder when we think of what we have lost
Over the years
And the universal language that united us
As one people
That his music brought,
Now in far flung corners we listen to the music of our homeland
And remember in the golden days
How we danced in the sun
To the one we called Tuku
His music made us feel happy
It made us feel sad
Mesmerised us with his dancing,
This gentle giant with his guitar
Who came seeping into our consciousness
With those twangy notes
And signature cough,
Every song told a story,
Go well Tuku
We will remember you
Zimbabweans across the globe bid you farewell
And shed tears
For all those happy years
You entertained us

With your incredible talent.
Gone, he is gone
And angels await at the gate
To welcome him home.

(On the passing of Oliver Mtukudzi)

One foot in front of the other

Put one foot in front of the other,
Forget about the pain that burns inside
Forget about Mama crying in the night
Forget about the fear in your heart
And the shadows where you cower and beg the soldiers to stop
Forget about the ripping apart
The fire between your legs
The force
The feel of a heavy hand around your neck
And the bruises and cuts
And the violation of your small person
Mama didn't give permission
For them to take
What belonged only to your father
The bride price he paid
The vows said on the Bible
In the sanctity of church,
Your white confirmation dress,
You did not give permission
For them to take your innocence
As you said a silent prayer to Jesus,
What choices have you had?
What bright future have you got?
Little girl in the dark
Desperate cries in the night
Weren't they meant to protect you?
Forget the sick feeling in your belly
The emptiness
The sorrow in your heart

Your tear-stained cheek,
Forget your searing terror
Every time a man passes your house,
The unstoppable thudding in your chest,
Like a broken clay pot
You may be able to hold the fragments in your hands
But can you ever put them back together?
Oh girl child
My heart weeps for you
As I hold my head in shame
For what I cannot change,
Put one foot in front of the other
As we shed our silent tears
For you
Our future, our progeny
Our destiny,
And watch this dark cloud descend
And pin a black heart to our breast
Until the world sits up and takes notice
Of the human rights that have been violated
In a little country in southern central Africa
Where the lives of innocent children and women have
very little value.

A place called home

It's been fifteen years, dear love
Do you miss me at all?
The pictures that hang on my wall
Speak to me of other places
Other faces
And yet I know that in my heart you dwell
Is this what it means to be in hell,
To close the door
And see you no more,
No more time to spend
Our hearts to rend
No more gardens to tend
Or post cards to send,
The family is all grown
Packed their bags and left home
You wouldn't know them now
Those children you showed how
Its disbanded
It started as soon as we landed
This growing apart
This new start
This bid to survive
To discover ourselves,
It was gradual at first
But became apparent as time moved forward
It was just too awkward
We had all in some way changed
We had lost the adhesive
That precious glue,

That kept us together
Kept us with you
I'm getting used to the empty space
And coming to terms
With the idea
That my feet may never
Walk in that place
And so I ask you
Do you remember my face,
Before I left to live in the west
And to push myself with the rest
To the ultimate test
Of tenacity
Could I survive without you ?
And as I continue to ponder
And roam
Anchor-less and mostly lost,
I find myself missing
The place I call home.
Yes, it's been fifteen years my love,
And much has changed
But some things stay the same
And it there is only one name
That is engraved
In that little space
That's called my heart.

Justice for Zimbabwe

The voice of the people
Is hardly heard these days
For fear of reprisals
From the strong arm of the military forces
Bulldogs of the regime
Propping up a geriatric junta
While the walls of Rome crumble into dust and desolation,
Gone are the glory days
When the voice of the people
Spoke for democracy
Liberty,
Freedom,
For many years now it has been used in vain
Blamed for rigged elections,
As weapon against the very people it is said to speak for,
How can it be heard
Amidst the shooting
And the shouting
And the battering of bodies and brains
Where even a whisper heard in the wrong dark corner
Can lead to arrest,
Torture
Death,
The stories have become distorted
The truth is a lie
And democracy is now just a meaningless word
In a world where there are no choices,
The people say one thing,
The powers that be say another,

But who pays the price
For the parties
The extravagance
The opulence?
Surely the people have a right to have their voices heard?
Human Rights
What does it mean?
Who gives one right to take away the right of another?
We were all born equal
In the eyes of the law we should all have the same protection,
Why is it that we don't ?
Why have the scales of injustice tipped so favourably in the
direction of the oppressor?
Powerless we hide
With bent knee and subservience
We cower and hope we are not seen
Where raising a head above the parapet is fatal
where only the invisible survive.
Do we go on suffering
While the guilty go unpunished,
Where is their retribution,
The day of reckoning?
When is our day in the Hague?
How many more years will it take
To stem the flow of blood
That gushes out of this gaping raw wound?

Of dust and dreams

When we were children a long time ago,
We'd pile into the *bakkie*
And head to the *bhundu*
The dam and the acacia trees were calling,
The deck chairs came out as dad walked down to the water
To fish for our supper
My dog, Charlie and I were in seventh heaven
Disappearing into the bush,
For hours leaving our paw prints in the sand of a dusty path,
A myriad of birds overhead,
Ceaseless cicada noises in our ears,
Netting tadpoles for a glass jar,
And dad telling me to throw back the tiddlers,
The afternoon swim
Pretending we were escaping from crocodiles
The labrador who wouldn't leave my side,
And sitting on a sheet of canvas rolling balls of *sadza pap* in the
palms of my dirty hands
Relish and *nyama*
Running down my chin
The little transistor radio
Belting out the Lyons Maid hit parade,
John Edmond
And how we all knew the words of Salome, Jennifer and me
Because that was the story of our lives
Jessica Jones,
Waikiki Man, Sunday, Monday, Tuesday,
Gwynneth Ashley Robin
Little Soldier Blue

And we remembered my brother who was fighting for his
country,
Far from the bosom of home,
To keep us safe
And although there were troubles
And sorrow
And we didn't know what would happen tomorrow
Our childhood days we full of sunshine
My toys were things I found in the bush
Sticks and stones
Bits of fishing line,
Mom producing two bags of sweets for our weekend treat,
Lemon and lime sherbets were the best
And chocolate éclairs
Because we shared the bag between us
And now when I think of those days,
The bush paths that are the atlas of my little lost soul,
And how I have managed to navigate my way to the other side of
the world,
Loosened the ties of my heritage,
Disintegration of family
In this dystopian lifestyle
Our memories blown away by the wind,
And I find myself alone,
I close my eyes and remember a night when we stood out on the
open plateau
And counted a thousand stars in the dark of an African night.

A letter of love to my birth country
Zimbabwean Independence Day, 18th April

I would gladly give you all my heart
But someone has a prior claim
She always did
From the very beginning
And even though she has changed her name a few times
Her heart has always been mine
As mine is hers,
And I never thought there'd come a time when we would be parted
But none of us can see into the future
Or know what destiny has in store for us
And this is probably as well,
I was happily settled
Had it all planned out,
Then came the day
When doubts clouded my mind
And there were futures
Other than my own to consider,
A terrible decision to face,
And a wrenching apart
Of two hearts
Mine and hers,
Walking away
Deserting sacred ground,
Never to be reconciled
Things that have tortured and contorted my brain
Ever since
Leaving me searching to find someone or something
to fill the gaping gulf of loss

And an empty feeling of displacement
that never quite leaves one's soul at peace,
Most days I am fine
I keep it on the periphery,
Wrapped in the beauty of this new place,
But then like a beast lurking in the dark shadows
Waiting to leap out
When I least expect it
It claws at my heart,
Surprise, it's form of attack,
Leaves me feeling defenceless
and fatally wounds me once more
Leaving me drowning in a sea of grief.
Before, I was different
Teacher, lover, blazer of the trail
Hoping to right the wrongs of the past
She gave me all these things
When we saw in the dawn of that new day,
Burning like the sun
With optimism,
But that can never be me
Not now,
That sixteen year old in 1980,
I am a remnant of my former self,
Life however, has shallower compensations
Things are simpler
And I'm learning to appreciate solitude
The life of an exile is a lonely one
Faced with the eternal question
Will I ever belong again?
Are my glory days behind me,

In another life, this was a given,
She never made me feel like this
Cast adrift
And so as another year passes
On this day of all days
Independence Day
I remember her once more
And toast her memory
And wonder if she will ever really be free,
Or is she cursed
Just like me?

African child with feet in sand

How you traversed this dusty land
When morning first heralded
it's eternal adventure
How you leapt from your bed
And walked into the sun
Feeling it's warmth so red,
And through the dewy grass you tread
Feeling the earth,
through your bare feet
Where spirit and nature meet
That's how you learned about your world
As everything was unfurled,
Before you knew the words
You heard the birds
That called "Go Away! Go Away!"
And this was yours,
All these were your days,
With stick in hand you poked the anthills
Toyed with the centipede
Knocked the fruit from the trees
Sucked the sour slippery taste of the marula
And the baobab seed
Chewed the sugar from the cane
And stole the mangoes
Again and again
And still the world was kind
And Mother Nature didn't mind
For you were her child,
And clambering up the rocks

Like a baboon,
You took the skin off your knee
But when you got up there
What could you see?
The master of all you survey
Out there it lay
This bushveld
This land
This moment yours,
And your heart was filled
With everything you had
For what else did you need?
And she gave you everything
Your first rememberings
Beauty beyond compare
And you kept it all
Saving the memories without even realising it
Oh barefoot Africa child
With the dust on your feet
And the sun on your skin,
But time plays funny tricks
And too soon the years pass by,
And now when you think of it
All you can do is cry,
And when it gets too much to bear,
You think of her standing there
Looking out across the void
That bridges yesterday and tomorrow
And you remember with sorrow
When this was all yours
When you held this treasure

And you thought you could keep it,
Not imagining for one minute
That history would sever
You and the land forever.

The first rains

(Harare 1984)

I ran and danced barefoot in the rain
He watched me while I washed my hair
With the pure water from the gutter pipe
And I shivered in its coolness
We laughed like children
Happy and filled with overwhelming joy
That the heavens had blessed us
After seven years of hard drought,
We heard it on the news
The dam was spilling over its wall,
Leaping into the car
We drove out to see for ourselves,
Cars lined the both sides of the road
All the city's residents had gathered
And we joined the throng
Posed for pictures
Asking random strangers to capture the moment
He laughed with a passer-by
No more water rationing
Water is life!
And we can begin again
To build our castles,
We stood by the dam wall
At the water's edge
Watching the power of the rapids,
Holding hands
Feeling the magnitude of our passion
I have those pictures still

My keepsake of the day,
You in your shorts and cap
Looking cool,
Me, sundress and giggles,
Although I have to blow the dust of thirty years off the album
They still make me smile
And I remember a time when we were young
When we walked in a dream
When money was tight
But we lived on the essence of pure love,
Our neighbours were our friends
And we played football with the children on lazy warm
afternoons,
Tinned bully beef suppers,
And later that night,
After we had made love
I lay in the crook of your arm,
As we fell asleep
Listening to the rain drops falling on the tin roof.

Beggars and exiles
(On the death of Mugabe)

I write this for my fellow country men, women and children…

Oh, the time has finally arrived
The day of reckoning
The day when you face your maker,
I hope you cower before him
In shame
For all the dishonour you have brought upon the children
of Zimbabwe,
What legacy to leave behind you!
Imagine how you will be remembered by history?
You, who tried to rewrite it
You, who took and green and living thing,
A people literate and strong,
A growing, thriving economy
Full of industry and hope,
And waved your clenched hand
And said this is mine!
Pamberi!
But it was one step forward and ten steps back
You, who spoke against colonialism
And then made our country a satellite of China,
And in less than four decades
Turned us all into beggars and exiles
While you wreaked a horrible reign of fear and terror
Over us all,
Dividing us with your hateful rhetoric,
And the land which you grabbed for your inner echelons,

The elections you blatantly rigged time and time again,
Stealing everybody's right to choose,
And the opposition you killed off,
Biting the hands that fed you
And sending farmers running
paralysed with fright for their lives,
While you butchered what was left,
Leaving people on their knees with starvation and dread,
While you ate cake,
A cake so big it could have fed us all,
And the silent ghosts who haunt the mine shafts and mass graves
where you threw their bodies
They will rise up and demand retribution
Children, you turned into orphans and prostitutes,
Animals you sold to the point of extinction
Our national parks you gave away wholesale to foreign eastern
nations
To pay for your greed and crippling debt
While you lined your pockets and those of your closest allies,
Your smug arrogance
Your nepotism
Corruption
pounded a jewel to dust
While your cronies fought over the spoils,
I will not weep a single tear
Or shout in jubilation
at your passing,
For we have all lost what we most treasured
Our birth right
And this has done us more damage than anything you could
ever imagine,

You departed this mortal world a tired and sick man,
What have you got to show
for the masquerade?
The so-called champion of the people,
Who was so terrified of his own shadow he travelled by
motorcade
And surrounded himself with brutal armed thugs
And now your era is over,
You will not be celebrated as some glorious ruler,
Some African Messiah,
The returning conquering hero,
You didn't know the meaning of the word,
And when your statue lies rusted and defiled
We too will remember the dictator who will not be revered
as a victor
But as a bloodthirsty murdering coward
And a very cunning jester
Who beguiled us all.

Rosen

Sometimes I sit in the silence of the moment
And think...
The sun is shining and the birds are singing
And I could almost be there...
Almost,
Sitting in the solitude of a shady veranda
Just us two,
Listening to your stories,
About your children in the rural area,
And how your mother is looking after them,
Polishing the floor red with cobra polish and pride,
From old knees well accustomed to hard labour
Arms that scoop me up
And carry me
A child high with fever
Who chides me when I'm cheeky
And who takes me kicking and screaming for my bath
When all I want to do is sit on the *stoep* and eat mangoes
Who gently combs my tangles
And plaits my hair in pretty braids
Who put the first ball of *sadza* and gravy into my little hand
And gave me my first taste of sorghum beer,
Who pushed me on a tyre swing
And promised not to tell mom when I did wrong,
Who kept all my secrets
And took the blame for all the broken things,
Who sang all my lullabies in Ndebele
And taught me my first words
That shaped my tongue to make clicks and clacks of the vernacular,

Who waited for me at the school gate
And who covered for me when I was late
Out longer than I should have been
And the street lights had been on longer than my curfew,
The person who stood between my mother and I
And saved me many a beating
Who carried love in her heart for me
As if I was her own
Who watched me grow
Introduced me to Jesus
And made me cry when I told a lie,
Gave me gifts of sugar cane,
Baobab pods,
Homemade peanut butter
And filled my days with her earthy presence,
Sitting side by side on the rug
Watching black and white TV late into the night
When the parents were out,
Falling asleep leaning into her for warmth,
Doorstep sandwiches, Sun Jam, mugs of tea made with
condensed milk,
Wrapping her mouth with a rag rather than go and face the dentist,
Who saw me through the pains of adolescence
And who left us when my mother thought I no longer needed a maid
She wasn't my nanny
She was my guardian, my confidante, my friend,
A constant mother who filled an empty gap
When mine was doing more important things,
I was her responsibility
I am her legacy
The person I am today because of her,

How many sons and daughters
Did our African mothers (and fathers) shape?
What would you make of us now
I wonder?
I hope I've made you proud
I have travelled far from the bosom of your love,
And sometimes
Just sometimes I could be there...
Well almost.

2

Devonshire

Blessed Easter Sunday

When the sun kisses the meadow and
It in turn smiles back
in a luminous green reflection of its love;
When the daffodils spread out their joyful greeting on the
roadside verges
And the primroses breakout into riotous abandonment on the banks;
When the purple haze of in a secluded forgotten corner of a
woodland walk
Suddenly makes you stop and draw breath;
And shepherds return careworn from endless nights of lambing;
And the village church bells beckon you to worship on this
beautiful and precious of all mornings
Then you will know it is Easter Sunday!
For the resurrected saviour
Has risen
And our sins have been forgiven.
Thank you for this day
And for showing us the way.
Hold your dear ones near
The Lord has taken way all fear
Rejoice and celebrate
For he has led us out of the darkness
And into the light of his grace.

Up on the moors

We sat side by side
I placed my head upon his lap
And he, looking down at me with love-filled eyes
Here where the placid waters flow
We lay on the bank like children
Lost in our green willows and moss covered stones
Where tame ponies roam
Not far from home,
For prehistoric mingles with ancient and Neolithic
Feeling like an eternal traveller
Time stands as still as the forests and the stones surround us,
I fear for the shaggy sheep who venture
too near to the road
Their wool caught on the rough wire hooks on the fences,
And the warning to motorists to mind out for the animals
The cattle grids and the those who do take extra care
Then there are the others who do not.
Weekenders, holiday pirates that treat the place like a race track
Those who do not know
That this is a precious space.
For me it is my soul's retreat -
A place of escape in a crazy world
Where I can wander around in the beauty
or just sit and listen to the music of wind blowing through the trees.
We come together,
The sky and I
He and me,
We meet here often
Like lovers in secret out in the open

And yet in seclusion,
I bathe my forehead in the coolness of the stream
All my worries
Flowing away over the rocks and under the bridge
And I, the lone figure
Stand to look at the rapids
And the watch families picnicking on the bank,
He sends me a wave and mock salute among the clouds
I point at the Mr Whippy Van and he nods
Then later walking by the reservoir
We venture down the path
While I test his knowledge on the fauna
With the questions posted on the signs
He never answers but he knows,
Enveloped in our green serene of wild fern,
heather and the heath
Mottled lichen spattered rocks, look like children have been let
loose with straws and brightly coloured paints.
Old stone circles up on high ledges,
Monuments to bygone age, hold our fascination
An undercurrent of the supernatural.
Refreshed, revived, replenished,
With every inhalation of clean air
My desire to return to the city totally diminishes.
How intertwined our lives have become
Like the twisted oaks where the wild pixies frolic in the stillness
of the green places
We cannot traverse the slippery stones
For fear of a broken ankle
So the pixies must get up to their tricks alone
But we can gaze into their space and marvel at their world.

How else to revive troubled souls but to spend time out here
alone us two
In the eerie shadows away from the sunlight under the canopy of trees
Where our spirits can run free
But mind you don't step on the Sun-before-Father, or the rheum
will soon be upon thee.
This is how I'd like to slip away one day;
Not in a wooden crate in some forgotten corner
Wondering why my friends were too busy
To say farewell to an old pal
As the hearse drives my coffin sombrely away.
No, give me a magnificent send-off
Looking at the sky
Surrounded by the majestic ash trees
Then let my spirit ascend and fly with the falcons.
If I am to exit this world let me do it in splendour, in magnificence,
Gazing up not down
With birds, not worms
Let me look down at a purple carpet of heather
Or see the wild daffodils
Not in some hospital taking a pill
Let me go as I have lived
Drawn to the tors
Up here on the moors.

On the train again

Heading home
Loved ones left behind
How I love to see them
Smiles and happy moments shared
And as the train rattles on towards my destination
Passing through the stations
I know so well now
We hug the Dawlish coast
I can't see it for the darkness
But I know it's there
Welcoming me home,
Newton Abbot and finally
Exhausted I arrive in Totnes
Hopping off the train to the warm centre of South Devon
And driving on to Kingsbridge,
Mixed emotions
Heavy heart,
Missing them already
But I'm coming back home
To where I'm led every time
The estuary and the bridge.
Where I live.

I often visit Torcross in my dreams

Taking me back to a scene I've captured many times in my
memory and on my camera.
Looking out toward the lighthouse across the bay
So close but seemingly far away
And to the other side where the barriers hold back the grasping
hands of the sea.
On Slapton Sands,
the ice cream van, the monument.
Torcross and the tank with garlands of poppies remembering the
fallen heroes of the last world war.
The fishermen with their windswept hair sticking up in the salty air
Rods in a line on the shingle
Remnants of broken net caught up in jagged shells
Half broken crabs petrified by the elements
The sea spinach growing on the fringes of the coast
And the gulls hovering just above
Waiting to sup on innards of the catch.
The silver blue multitude flying through the waves.
White pebbles polished smooth
And driftwood roughly edged and awaiting beach combers or the
tide to reclaim it.
 The children with bucket and spades
 Wading in the translucent light of the water.
Aromas of fish and chips suppers from the restaurants fill the air
and the belly with longing.
The buoys like beachballs bobbing on the top look like lost
swimmers trying hard not to go dancing under.
Out on the point
A walk pleasant under April skies

Where bluebells cling to the sides of the cliff in desperate devotion,
Fighting for a space among the gorse and fern.
In the summer months
You could be forgiven for thinking you had landed in heaven.
So, forward to the edge
And the towering lighthouse beacon,
Casting a daunting shadow in the sunlight
But in the darkness, a beam of hope
through treacherous storms.
With arms out stretched from east to west
I feel like a child, insignificant
Under this vast expanse of sea and sky
It's magnitude magnificent it takes away my breath with its beauty.
And so I amuse the child with possibilities.
"If you jump in to the sea and swim in that direction you'll end up in France."
She stares at me with wonder.
Imaginations fired, mine included.
 Is it really that easy to escape?
 To swim and never look back?
 Imagine making it to the other side
 The shear exhilaration of the thought makes me shudder.

A rain-washed night in Devon

You, my dear, will live forever
For I have loved you.
I dressed you up in words
Cloaked you in magic
Surrounded in mystique
In my verses you are wise
You are kind
Your smile opened a window so wide
The whole universe came in
It reached in and transported me
To the lands you took me to
Every song, every poem, every time you laugh,
All those colours
The food we tasted
The conversations we had
And the way you made me feel
The love I felt for you
The soft and gentle longing
Listening to you breathe in the dark
In my dreams, in my head, in my heart
You come to me
Sweetly to my door
It's always open, I'm always here
And maybe on a night like this
When the rain is reflected in a pool of light on the road
And the music plays on to the lonely lover
Who waits in hope
You will forget to protest
and lose yourself completely

in my arms
And we will stop trying to find reasons
Not to
Worrying about what will happen tomorrow
And what others think
For it will not matter
Because everything we need
Will be right in front of us.

Scene from a west Charleton window

I reached out for my paints and coloured the sky blue
Smudged out the grey in the day
The shadows in the trees.
In between the bare branches I painted verdant vivid green leaves
And the grass was teeming with flowers
And bubble-bees
And the birds had not left
To enjoy a vacation on southern shores.
Summer fruit dropped into my lap
And as I turned up the heating in my flat and my bright lamp to
chase away the dark
I put on my floppy hat
And drank a glass of super-charged orange juice with a Lemsip
And tried to avoid the barrage of colds and sniffles at every
corner
I tried to forget that the Earth was turned in a sulk away from
the sun
And the prospect of the miserable months ahead
Where I willing go into hibernation and become a mole
Scuffling about in the gloom
And that my friends in the southern hemisphere are waking up
to a beautiful morning
Sweeping jacaranda blossoms from their driveways
And having iced drinks by the pool for breakfast
I closed my eyes just for a moment
And visualised the warmth of an African day
And wish myself away.

On arrival

Stepping off the plane
To a blanket of rain
Bristol Airport looked small
Or so I thought,
A similar sized airport to that in my own home town, Bulawayo,
Now in a life, a million miles away,
But I was travel worn,
You see I'd never left Africa
Not since I was born.
And now in my fortieth year
I was shell-shocked, exhausted from the flight
And the uncertainty of what lay ahead,
My heart was breaking from the very thought of it.
Uncle was waiting
Trailer at hand,
To take charge of this unhappy band
Of relies he'd never met,
The hightailing down the motorway
I'll never forget,
As Uncle put his foot down.
And I tried to take in a water-washed Somerset.
I felt sick, I felt green,
But Devon was the most beautiful place I'd ever seen,
Uncle turned off into the lanes,
I hope I never have that experience again!!
The hedgerows, tunnel vision and Uncle's driving skills
Provided the backseat passengers with white knuckle thrills
But for me, I needed to puke!
A detour to South Milton Sands

The children had never seen the sea
Photos and smiles on the beach
But not for me.
All I wanted to do was reach
And so I sat cradling my head by the roadside
While they looked at the in-coming tide.
Another hairy ride through the lane
With Uncle back at the wheel again,
Heaven help anyone coming the other way!
They'd have to reverse into a bay,
And so we arrived at Libertas
Aunty waiting to welcome us
With warmth
As away to bed I went
To nurse my nausea and splitting head.
Once the rain had cleared
And the sun had once again reared
We soaked up the beauty of the garden,
And the Indian summer that followed
That first August and September,
And so it was that I remember,
That five frightened Africans
Boarded that plane
Never to see Zimbabwe again.
It's been fifteen years
And I've cried a bucket-load of tears
But I've also laughed and loved
And learnt to live again,
I left a family to find a family
And lost a home to gain one
Our little band has gone its separate ways

Evolved and changed
Each in their own style
We meet up once in a while
But we're certainly not who we once were,
As for me, I think of Africa often,
More than there are hours in the day,
I've come a long way,
And on days I feel blue,
I pick up my pen and write my lines to you,
Who first gave me life
As I pass these memories to a new generation,
Who will never know where we come from.
Now I'm part of the fabric that makes up our little town in the
South Hams,
So I'd like to say thank you to Kingsbridge
You've been a pal
And treated me well
And although I'm not quite considered a local
I'm getting there slowly in my own pace
Because that's how we do it here in this place,
You're getting the measure of this maid
Who, one strange and rainy day, came to stay.

Autumn English roses

I passed by your house today
In the village where you used to live,
And it made me sad to think you were no longer there,
All was tranquil in the early autumn sunshine,
Mild weather for October,
Roses climbing up the trellises
Still giving off their last desperate perfume,
Your hydrangeas were just fading from pink to a more duskier hue,
And I thought about the first day we met
Your request to my husband's aunt
to meet the family from Africa,
And how in those first few days
When I walked around in a confused daze
You took me under your wing,
My first English friend,
Well-travelled, sophisticated, interesting,
Who took my arm
And walked with me in the lanes
Your spaniel bounding ahead,
And I was reminded of the first summer
And then later when your daughter came to stay
And our girls were new-made friends,
And how we nurtured our little roses,
Yours, a carefree gypsy spirit,
And mine, quiet and shy,
Your rose was always first to leap over a gate, fall in the mud,
race into the water,
Devour a bag of sweets,
And mine with her crystals

and books;
And how you two twirled around the room singing arm in arm,
And how I watched wishing my daughter and I could do the same,
Drinking elderflower pressé in your garden in summer,
The girls squabbling over the last Jaffa Cake,
Our attempts to mould them
To tame them
To prepare them to do something sensible,
I think I trained mine too hard,
Wanting her to conform
But she will have none of me now,
And has gone her own way,
Strange how they've ended up at the same college
Probably passing each other by each day
Neither acknowledging the playmates they were
Many summers ago;
And the men we loved who infuriated us,
They are both gone now,
And when my first winter came,
And we sat sipping rosé in the warm glow of the firelight,
I remember how giggly you got as we shared life's loves
And losses,
I never had a friend who wanted to drink wine with me before,
I learned a lot from you in those early days
When my heart was still numb
From the loss of losing my country,
You showed me there was a life after,
Encouraging me to come out
For walks at Gara,
And over the fields
And that there was beauty right here,

You treated me like an equal,
Looking beyond my awkward foreignness
And being a real friend.
As the leaves start to fall and change
I contemplate how I'm the only one left,
You call another place home now,
And the girls too have gone,
No longer our responsibility,
We can never have those days back again, my friend,
And I watch the last of the petals fall and scatter in the rough
cold winds.

Grey around the bay

It's grey around the bay today
As the steely sky meets the jade sea
The white crests of the waves
Catch the light
That's trying to break through
And there's no holiday makers today
The grockles are all far away
Cream teas and seaside breakfasts
Won't be served,
And so we watch from train windows
At the men on the golf course
And the unpeopled boats,
Harboured for now
As they wait for their return,
It's a peaceful day in Devon,
The caravan park is quiet
And there are no camper vans on the roads,
It's a day to exhale
A day to take stock
The air is a little cooler
Much needed respite from the heat,
And as we go
We go slowly
And take in the view
No need to rush
We don't need to make a fuss
For this is the place
We call home
Visitors are welcome

There's a time and a place
But once they've all gone home
We slip back into our ways
And rest a pace
Let them return to the rat race,
We lend them some time
And a little of our space
Yes, do come for a holiday
But this is our place.
And here where the air is clear
And the beaches clean
It is the best place you've ever seen
This our Devon
And our little piece of heaven.

Crazy, carefree, young things

When the heat of summer is at its height
And the warmer weather reminds us of childhood days,
I see the youngsters of the town flocking in the direction
of the bridge
Their lean, brown athletic bodies
Perch on the edge
As they vault themselves off
plummeting into the water
I pass them on my way home from work
And they beckon to me to sound the horn
I do and I wave to these blithe young birds
Some motorists find them a hazard
On so narrow a bridge
Some think their exploits precarious,
But I think they are magnificent!
Beautiful young things
Carefree and fearless
I admire their bravado
And joyous abandon
They are not hostile to those of us who drive safely around them
It must be wonderful to live in the moment
Grabbing life with every exaggerated leap into the murky water.
I think I have almost forgotten how,
I remember a time when I too
Jumped into depths unknown
And swam fearless of crocodiles and water snakes
In a country and continent
Far away from our Devonshire shores.
I remember the feeling of freedom

Thinking that I was invincible,
Alone, save for my dog,
I would venture away from the gathering and dive off a rock.
How empowering it felt to have the whole dam to myself!
And the days when I rode off to the game park on a bicycle
Sometimes with a friend
Sometimes by myself.
Gone are those days of youthful exuberance
Now I walk with a stoop
And feel pains in my joints,
But my, those were the days!
And so this evening when I saw them there
I smiled and called out to them
For today is all they have
And so we must let them be.

Royal wedding

On a beautiful day in mid-May
The world gathered around the House of Windsor
Seas of joyous faces
Red, white and blue
Lining the Long Walk
The fairy-tale princes cut a dash
In blues and royals
Amid the tiers of roses
In the carved and ornate beauty of the chapel
And the pews were crammed with the bold and the beautiful
One past Prime Minister;
The golden man of football
David Beckham;
And a tennis legend Serena Williams;
Actors and actresses
Gorgeous George
And a little glimpse of the heavenly Idris
Oh my, oh me!
As we held a collective breath
Would she wear white or a shade of ivory?
And at the West Gate
All eyes on our new princess
And our hearts wept for the angel
Who could not be there
And how we all remember that heart-breaking image of a twelve
year old son
And the passing of his mother
How proud she would have been of her lads
Handsome and regal

Every inch the royal princes that they are
And heaven is smiling
On this most precious of days
And then our most glorious Majesty
A vision in lime green and floral purple
And also the mother of the bride
With quiet dignity
What a proud moment for any mother
And a clutch of precious ones,
flower-girls and pages
Who stole the show
Little rays of sunshine
Garlands of roses
And then our bride arrives!
Simply elegant
And she enters
To a fanfare
And walks alone with the children
Takes the arm of Prince Charles
Radiant,
Not a dry eye in the house
Or in homes across the world,
God is love.
And so it begins
From now and till ever after
Two hearts entwined
Her hand resting on his knee
His hand enveloping hers
Little acts of affection
And the gospel choir sang
And their faithfulness was sealed

And the young girls wept
Both princes betrothed
Both princes wed
To love and to cherish
And so it was that it was
And so we wish them a lifetime of happiness
Harry and his princess
Meghan and her prince
Let the light of your love
Illuminate the darkness
In a world of disappearing values
Hold it high
For all to see.
For now,
For always.
For love conquers all.

A January morning in South Devon

The moon was showing the water her beauty
as I crossed the bridge,
And the waves were grateful
For they would never have known such luminosity
Without her glittery magnificence touching their surface.
As I drove out of Kingsbridge town
Clouds were smudging the dawn sky with grey finger prints.
The branches of road-side trees stretched their naked boughs
Shivering in the damp morning air
By the time I had reached the station
Darkness had lifted its lid
To a beautiful and fine morning
A coverlet of soft green covered the fields
Between Totnes and Teignmouth
The sun had arisen in all her splendid glory
Cinnamon clouds framing the blue
Along the Dawlish coast line
Over the water Exmouth draped in a golden glow
Little deer wandered near the castle on the right side of the train
Power lines left marooned in the flooded plain
Stood looking bewildered.
The red bricked buildings of Exeter welcomed us
And the humans came and went
Jumping off the train
Scurrying along the platform clutching their lattes
Buying newspapers
Leaping on board
Mobile phones grafted to the palm of their hands,
The relentless tapping of their forefingers

Returning to work after the Christmas break
Looking glum
Putting on their exterior masks
To face the world,
And I returned to my occupation
And stared out of the window.
And far away over the hills
The moon just dissolving in the sky
Was saying goodbye.

To Devonshire with love

With a sore and fragile heart
Did I come to you
To make a new start
And with arms opened wide
You took me in
A traveller from half the world away
Who came to settle,
Who came to stay,
In the country villages
Where people
Local and steadfast
Watch the comings and goings
With interest and trepidation
Cautiously taking strangers in,
I came to lay my weary, careworn spirit.
A man from across the way
Walked over, touched my shoulder and said
"Don't worry maid, you'll be accepted
Once we get the measure of you."
And I have to say this was true.
And now I find myself saying
"Where've you been to?"
Devonshire, like the beautiful lane flowers,
Slowly and gently washed over me
And stilled my aching heart,
Her beauty she showed me in my weakest moment
The soft light on a distant field in early March
When I last heard my mother's voice on the phone
As she slipped into the arms of the angels

Ten thousand miles away in South Africa,
And when we scattered a beloved mother in law's last remains
into the sea,
On a cold January morning,
Missing the opportunity to hold hands at the bedside of the
departing ones,
In that secluded corner in a quiet spot
Is where I find my peace.
My heart is lightest when the blossoms arrive
After a long winter
And looking up into the canopy
I am wrapped in splendid green
Fresh and verdant,
The cry of a pheasant
Leaping out of a hedgerow
Beautiful scenes of red campion and bluebells that grow
side by side
And the poppies in early May
These things take my breath away.
Travelling home along the estuary
Over Bowcombe
Looking at the water
Gives me such a restful feeling
Where the children throw themselves over the bridge
On warmer evenings, diving into the murky depths below
And where I have paddled in a canoe
Quite happily.
Matthew's Point and the views of the sea
From Dartmouth to Slapton
I cannot help but feel
That life gives us all a second chance

And it's not what it seems at first glance
I am thankful and I am grateful for the welcome you've given.
I wasn't born here
But I was led here
And now I know why
For my heart, like the patchwork fields
Has been stitched back together
One piece at a time
And so I offer you my gratitude
For giving me fortitude
And the strength when I could not go on
To look over a gate and see the vistas
I have seen,
This is my idea of heaven
My idea of perfection
Beautiful, glorious Devon.

For Leia

She followed me up the stairs the night my great aunt died
I was sad, I felt a great spirit had ascended
I felt alone
And far from home
But she just knew
Such a comfort
She slept beside me,
Purring in my ear
When my heart was sore,
Such a timid thing
She shied away from most
But to me she had attached
Herself,
She just knew,
I had been secretly feeding her from my store cupboard
Tuna and tinned sardines,
Tit bits here and there,
She wouldn't come when he called
Although she belonged next door,
She just knew.
One day a dog arrived
It sealed our fate,
She turned tail and ran into mine,
Where she remained by my side
Then the baby came,
By now it was noticed
I'd kidnapped his cat,
I'd taken her to the vet
Jabs and ointment for the fleas

He knocked on my door
"You may as well have her,
She spends all her time with you. We're moving anyway."
Somehow she just knew,
A house cat
I think not!
She ventured to spend more time outside
Presenting me with little creatures
Living and dead
I'm not one for mice
And I don't like bats
But my heart goes out to the little shrews
I tell her it's not right
And that she mustn't do it
But she just kncw,
And when a cat makes her home with you
There's nothing you can do
Accept the fact
She's here to stay,
She can see a softy from a mile away
And somehow she just knew!

Once upon an English May morn

Grey is the day
Wet are the roofs
Cold are my bones
Digits clenched with an icy fist
Heavy are the skies
Like the bags around my eyes
Sleep tempts me back to bed
But the day is not passed noon
And my day's work far from done
I long for the warmth of my cocoon
How much more pleasant the sound of the rain
When heard from the safe haven of my room
Laden is my burden
Tiresome is my toil
I slope in my chair like a slug
Contemplating my doom

The last day of August

When the passion of summer has run its course
And the roses of the sultry days begin to lose their petals
in the vase
The birds leave our shore and fly off in V formation
As we look up to the blue of the sky and photograph it in our
mind's eye
For those endless dull, heaven, leaden globes
That lay on our shoulders for the months ahead
We will pack away our bright cotton shirts, sun hats and flip flops
And bring out the woollen socks and double duvets and
crochet blankets
for when the nights begin to draw us closer to the hearth
And we will remember summer and lovers found and lost
And those we keep in our hearts
In spite of the hopelessness of it all.
Opportunities that fell in our laps
And those that passed us by
The exotic holidays and the ones spent in our backyards
The carefree feeling of days that lasted forever
And the nights we feel asleep with the lace curtain blowing
in the breeze
Cooling our skins
Windows thrown open in happy abandon
The starlight, the moon glow and dreams of warm romance
The things we did, the friends we made and promises not quite kept
Like children returning to school
we will go back to our toil, responsibility and mortgages
Smile a sad little smile
Sigh and say "Now that was a summer to remember."

Reflections on a wet August morn

Here we sit in our little flat,
I and the cat
We've hardly room to swing a mouse
In this poor excuse for a house
We're having a *staycation* this year
Watching the world from our window
With our TV suppers and reduced circumstances,
Well, we've had a lot to cope with
A lot to pay for and still it goes on
And heaven only knows where next year will find us,
But we get by, still we get by
With the help of counselling, self-soothing and mindful colouring
And while the ex is tripping the life fantastic
With new hairdos and Pride marches through the towns and the
parties and new identity,
We'll sit here and quietly contemplate life
And even though the offspring refuses to talk
And writing alimony cheques seem never ending
While the whole world goes mad
We will get by, still we'll get by.
And the Bank holiday weekend was superb
And the weather was uncommonly hot
But I was under a cloud of one of my terrible heads
Passing it in assimilated dark.
The cat came and went
I fed and let her in and out
in a daze of pills and pain
And on Monday when the malaise was slowly lifting
Laundry was attempted

I found neighbours making the most of it
Filling the courtyard with their laughter
neighbours, Karen and Neil dragging out the bike for a service
and a polish,
DJ Dave exercising his brightly coloured yellow snake
And a warning that it likes to appear in the strangest of places!
Roberta watering plants galore.
we spent a happy afternoon messing about on the bike
I managed 10 vigorous minutes
With Stephanie and Baby Fynn cheering on
Before I flagged out and retreated for apple, blackcurrant and soda
While Karen ploughed on relentless.
And we got by, still we got by.
And so, it is the simple pleasures that see us through
That and the treasure of real human connection
Friends and family who check on us daily
To see if we are coping
Visitors who drop by,
Reaching out, adding colour and conversation
And it's not about having money or watching the pennies or
waiting for the day when everything will be perfect
It's about taking today and making it the best possible day you can.
And saying to yourself ... and the cat
We are getting by, my goodness and how!!
Shall we celebrate? You can have some whiskers and I'll have the
last Rich Tea biscuit in the tin.

These four walls

These four walls have heard the desperate out pouring of my heart
They have heard my mirthering
And my twisting
At the injustice of it all,
And seen me on the carpet
In a heap of sorrow and what might have beens.
The early days weren't easy
But from the moment I first stepped through the door
I was welcomed and embraced by the space,
And I knew this place
Would be my haven.
These four walls have seen me grow
And they know
What it has taken to get me here today.
The anguish, worry, pain and joy.
It's not always neat and tidy
But it holds my most treasured things,
Photographs of my best beloveds,
My favourite books
Trinkets and memories of beautiful holidays,
Warm coloured rugs and throws
And when I walk through the Bedouin style drapes
I feel a peace descend,
I feel my influences
My African roots
Drums, instruments and dolls,
Places I have loved,
And those precious angels who watch over me.
I've had very few visitors

But those who have come
Came and bought their own special gifts
Of friendship and support.
Some would call it bijou
But when I came here it was everything I needed
To keep body and spirit together,
But now the mistress of the cat
Must find a new flat
For we have quite out grown the place!
So I want to thank you
For giving me a place to rest,
And for the calm solitude
Where I have been able to
Find healing,
And a dry ceiling,
Where I have written my poetry
And found a voice
When I had very little choice,
And so here's to thee
Four walls,
I hope you will offer sanctuary
To another wanderer
And one day when I'm famous
Or possibly notorious
We'll put a blue plaque
On the wall outside
And it will say the poet lived here with her cat
During the years of bread and soup.

The birds have flown south

The geese passed overhead in a perfect V formation
And seemed to call to me
So long, see you later
When the warm days return!
Their shadow sealed my fate
And now the interminable wait will seem forever,
I take myself off to the beach
To blow away the cobwebs
The hue of the sea is aquamarine
Not quite blue, not quite green
It is very troubled today
The waves impossibly high
But oh the calm as they break on the cobble
Translucent best describes it
As the foam spills over the soapsud-blue,
That particular shade
is my favourite colour
It has that unique quality about it
Not often seen
And only captured in water
It is transient
Ever changing
And only appears when the light catches it
Playing with it like a child plays with water in his hand,
I marvel at its beauty
Even in this weather
With these steel-grey clouds over head
As I am ravaged by the force of the wind,
And looking out over the crested breakers

I catch the line where the shallows meet the deep
And see the distinct shades
Of light and dark blue
And I am reminded of you
Far away in a sunny corner
Also on the edge of the ocean
But by warmer seas,
I will not surrender to the darkness
And retreat within
Though the bronzed metallic carpet beneath my feet
Is treacherous with every falling leaf,
As the trees are slowly stripped of their foliage,
No, I choose to be in the light
Even with the shortening of the days,
As we face the dark half of the year.
And with the birds
Go the people to find the eternal sun,
It's not such a bad thing to remain behind,
Those of us here
Must gather together
Find warmth as we huddle
And hunker down
To face another winter
With our northern aspect.

A call to war

There was a call to war
And brothers, fathers, uncles, cousins and grandfathers
Heeded the call,
To protect our land, our values, our lives
Children, parents, families and wives,
Some were innocent
Barely children themselves,
Your first born sons,
Your special ones,
Some were old dogs of war,
Battle wary
With scars and experience
They'd earned before,
And so they went forth
Into the heat, into the flies,
Into battle torn skies
To fight enemies unseen,
In the sweat of a savanna summer
In foreign fields of green
And their mothers and their sweethearts cried
In desperation
And kept them in their prayers
And down the months and years
We lament for marriages that never took place,
And for that empty space
At the dinner table,
For babies who never knew their dads
And for the families who buried what little they had
Of their last remains,

And so we thank them
These brave heroes of ours,
For the bullets they dodged
For the hunger that lodged deep in their bellies
And the building rage
And the silent tears they wept
Far from home
For brothers in arms
Who died before their eyes
For the fear they felt
And their lost youth
And for their precious lives,
We can never know the extent of what they endured
How their nerves were stretched to breaking point
Sleep-deprived eyes
Endless nights
Guarding, guiding, protecting
Brain-fogged by battle, dirt, mud, rats, snakes, disease,
Blood lost, limbs and minds
Crawling under wire that would peel the skin off your back
And landmines buried deep
Faces against dampened earth
Muscles and hearts
With no respite
On red alert
Day after day
Year after year
These were men, my friends,
Whose will to survive burned strong
Who saw terrible things
Until what was human of them

Was left in a forgotten corner of their minds,
And so we thank them
For their courage and tenacity,
Grit and brawn,
So we could have a bright dawn,
They fought for you
They fought for me
They gave themselves so we could be free
Respect their sacrifice and dedication
For everyone in this nation.

(100 year Celebration of Armistice Day)

He sat on the foreshore alone

Looking at something on his phone,
Woolly hat pulled over his ears
To keep out the cold
On this brisk November day,
As birds of the water swam by
And the boats lay tethered
Bobbing on the waves,
The wind chilly and building up to a hooley
The dry leaves scurrying across the road
Like runaway children,
I saw him as I came over the bridge
And I wondered how he could stand to sit with so much beauty
around him
And not take notice,
And how the business on his mobile
Could compete with all this,
And questioned why he was by himself,
Was it the solitude that brought him here
Or was he reaching out for someone on his device?
In this world of instant access
To ready-made friends
worldwide,
I wonder how many of us
Are on our own,
Our phones now our only point of contact,
Parents with children miles away
Loved ones detached
Families dysfunctional,
And I weep for the lonely

Amongst us,
Who bury ourselves in our phones, tablets and plug our ears with
headphones
To keep conversation out,
We should all wear signs
"Do not disturb – out for lunch."
In a planet over-populated by people
How insular we all seem,
Social media seems a poor substitute for real human contact
Proper human company,
And remembered reading about someone who married a
hologram,
A good looking young man
Who lived in Japan
He could easily have made someone happy
Instead he goes to bed with a rag doll
An effigy if his virtual wife,
How many of us live in a virtual reality,
I feel desperate for the human race,
With our avatars and online profiles,
What's wrong with our beautiful faces?
In this life where we live at such a fast pace,
And haven't got the time
To form meaningful relationships,
As we go about our daily lives
With all our trouble and strife.

How beautiful Devonshire looks in the sunshine!

White hawthorn blossoms welcome the weary traveller back
from lands afar,
And here am I with a spirit filled with gratitude
Richer for my experiences
Yet content to be returning to
my adopted place
My restless feet will always carry me far
But like a guiding star
My heart always brings me back
To your shores
To your moors
To your calm waters
Where I have anchored my desolate soul,
Back to the bloom-filled lanes
Spring time in Devon
Always makes me feel as right as rain
And I am content to be back here again,
And as I travel closer
To my journey's end
I think of all the explanations
Why I love you so,
My refuge,
My quiet harbour
My solitude
The peace that descends
At each day's end,
And although I love to roam
You always draw me home,

And I don't understand why,
But like the blossoms that return with the changing seasons,
I will always find the reasons
To return here,
To you.

Summer has given us the slip!

I hope she's only on a short break and not a full blown sabbatical,
Jumpers, gloves and socks
So carefully packed away in mothballs
Have been dragged out again
And all of summer's things are on hold
As their cheery colours wave back at me from hangers;
Out in the rain and the cold
We huddle in the bus stop for warmth
As June looks and feels more like November
Grey skies replace the blue
we knew last week
Our vibrant vitality dissipates
With the rain,
Water washed fields;
Skin that was slowly turning the colour of autumn berries is
covered now
And fated to fade to more muted hues
And the energy and optimism of the last few weeks
Disappears too.
Barbecues remain covered
The outdoor pool untouched
As we gather once more around the telly,
With hot water bottles in our warm winter gowns
Casseroles and dumplings for tea
No day trips to the sea,
Oh where has summer departed to?
As Gemini's children
dread wet and dreary birthdays
And how will we celebrate the moon

When solstice arrives soon?
She has fled, so it would seem,
Taking with her all our mid-summer nights' wishes and dreams!

My bridge

I live just over this bridge
And how I love the view
Every journey brings me so much closer to you
At the start of the day
I inhale the fresh morning air
As I make my way into the town
To face the working day,
But at night ...
Ah ...
That's when I exhale
All the stresses away,
It is my bridge
And I love the view
The boats on the water,
The summer's evening we sped across it in your sport's car
On the way to the coast,
The water that sleeps in the dew
And comes and goes
With the tide,
The sigh of soft waves
When all is calm,
The tempestuous fever
When the water is high,
And so it is with me
Depending on the mood,
We are at one,
This place and me,
They say you can't feed off the scenery
But I disagree

It nourishes my soul
All year round
Fills my heart with happiness
Contentment,
I love the sun through the trees
Just around the bend,
Honestly, it is like heaven to me,
I like it in all seasons
But in the summer
That's is when I like it the best,
This bridge knows all my secrets,
It hides all my lies
And it has heard my sighs
It knows how hard I try,
It feels my silent longing,
The want in my heart
And the feeling of belonging,
On moonlit nights
When I return after a long day's work
When I leave the town behind
And make my way back
Half blind from fatigue,
Ready to surrender to sleep
She is my comfort
Gently guiding me home,
Day and night,
I love this sight,
Yes, this is my bridge
And I live just over the ridge,
I love the view
Just like the way I feel about you.

Someone to share the view

It's the summer evenings I love the most
As birdsong continues till darkness wraps itself around us
And the fragrance of the first May roses
Fills the air with all the promise of romances,
And drifting into June
That's when I really start to swoon
As birthdays approach,
Oh happy are they who have reasons to celebrate,
Content am I to dream,
For I believe in love
I am defined by it
And being quixotic has never let me down
And as I climb to the heights both in my mind
And as I trundle up the moor,
The thought of you
Sits so comfortably
Between here and the blue yonder,
Perhaps we'll take the rug up there
One evening, you and me,
With a flask for our warm tea,
And just take in the view,
For now, at this present moment,
I am happy just to be,
As I collect blossoms for my rooms
And light my night-time fragrances
I lap up the last few minutes of soft light from outside
Whilst indoors lamps and candles coax me into a reverie
And the sweet soothing melodies ease the troubles
That have built up during the day

But now they slip away into the shadows
And loosen their grip as they diminish in size
And I let good feelings flow
And leave my thoughts to wander,
Pleasantly in my little daydream,
Yes, I love the summer evenings,
They are made for magic,
Fairy lights and love.

Just another half an hour

Please leave me to sleep
Oh dear pussy cat!
I just need five minutes more
And then up comes her paw
Softly, gently
Insistently
Touching my cheek
No claws,
Please cat
Don't do that!
Just one minute more
And turning over
I try to prolong my rest
But she does her best
And puts her ever-loving patience to the test
Time to get up!
Please dear little catkins
It's not even six yet
And as I drift off again
She ups the ante
Driving me completely scatty
Oh this little cat!
It's not breakfast she wants
Although she wouldn't mind
It's attention she seeks
Which is all fine and good
But I haven't slept all day
Quietly purring in a sunny corner
And these last precious moments

Are all I've got to sustain me through another bout of drudgery
But she refuses to go away
And so a reluctant hand reaches out to stroke her in the semi
light of early morning
Before the day is dawning
And then she is content
And we tick along,
She and I
This little pal
Who doesn't want a fuss
What a gal!
And so it is thus
Each morning of every day
She wakes me this way.

The hotel of dead bats

That darn cat has been at it again
Up all night on the hunt
Terrorising the little creatures that dwell nearby
Now she slumbers soundly
While I clear up the debris
I never know what I will awake to
And I must remember to always wear slippers
As I really don't fancy stepping in something squishy!
Laying there sound asleep
Butter wouldn't melt!
She was so affectionate last eve
Nestling into me for cuddles and strokes,
But when the moon is high in the sky
She leaps out of the window
And strikes
There were three dead bodies this morning
Strategically placed in my path
It's become an obstacle course just going to the loo
A bat, a field mouse and a little shrew
She's starting to stir
We will have words!
She eyes me apologetically,
Well you, young lady, are quite literally in the poo!
And don't look at me that way
You've had your fun
And you know what you've done!
No, don't wind yourself through my legs
And kisses are out of the question
And don't think for one minute I'm sharing my breakfast!

Salcombe meandering

What a walk is this
With a sky so blue it almost makes one sad
To think in a month or two
All this will be forgotten
A cabbage white flutters among the last of the valerian
Honey suckle perfumes the air
And down the hill
In the distance a beautiful view of Mill Bay,
And the summer boats;
The holiday makers pass me by
Plodding into town
To sit beside the water,
And enjoy the sun,
The heat is blistering today,
A lovely Bank Holiday Monday for a change,
The bees quite drowsy
But making hay while blossoms
Give a last desperate display
Before the chills of September
With its darker evenings
And colder mornings;
It's like summer is giving us one final blast
As I am only too aware
But for today, this afternoon,
Let's enjoy it
Make the most of it,
And tomorrow when we return to our toil
And focus our energies on more serious pursuits
We can file this one away

And dip into it
When our thoughts wonder back
To that glorious August day,
When all we had to do was soak up the sun.

3

Matters of
the Heart

The unobtainable rose

I've travelled half way across the world
Run away over the miles,
But nothing makes me think about home
Than when I look into your eyes,
The Devonshire coastline
On a cloudless day
Will always make me feel this way;
And now I find
The heart grows fonder
With the passing of every day
As I while away the hours
In comfortable repose
Thinking of that unobtainable rose,
Surrounded by brambles
I could never hope to tame
Lest I risk the pain
Of loss,
And I wouldn't for all the world
Hope to possess such a spirit
Wild and free,
And so I gaze on with a softness in my eyes
from the safe distance of firmer ground
Surrounded by the purple heather
And the yellow hedgerow furze
Primroses in abundance
Following close on the heels
Of the daffodils
And breathe deep the pure air of a spring day,
And as the snowdrops start to fade

To give way for bluebells
So must I retreat
As a shower starts to threaten
This beautiful scene
And as I round the bend
I am blessed with the vision of a rainbow
Over the fields,
And at its end
Maybe I will find a path
That leads to your heart.

Wistful love

I spent the whole of last year completely in love with you.
How can I now look at you with eyes anew?
As my pen bleeds on to the paper
Spilling out words I would never disclose
My heart beats once more with hope
Flooding those hidden desires into my veins
Oh sweet, secret love
How am I to cope
When I see you from afar
When I feel you close by
When your peals of laughter fall around me
Making me the giddy and silly girl that I am?
How do I show decorum
And pretend to be grown up and in control
When my fifty year old heart feels sixteen once more?
Am I not a piece of twine
And you the cat who toys with it
Pulling at my heart strings?
How can I waste another twelve month on this
Fitful wish that will vanish like the morning dew
With the coming of the sun?
Get thee gone and torment me no more.

The Southern African Lonely Hearts Club

Far away from home and single
I find myself once more looking for love,
Well, in my 50's what's a girl to do?
It is complicated over here.
First up, I don't speak the lingo
Well, I do and I don't
While English is my first language
And the subject I studied at uni and taught in a posh school in Africa,
I'm told I don't speak it correctly,
My accent is all wrong
My pronunciation is South African.
Let me state for the record
I am actually a Zim chick
So have no prior claim to belonging to the nation of rainbows.
And believe me, I've often had to draw a map!
Next thing, most daunting is body language
I'm getting it all wrong apparently,
I'm not supposed to flirt
I'm not supposed to be too forward
And wearing my heart on my sleeve is a definite no-no
Being a hopeless romantic is not helping the situation,
It's scaring them off in droves.
Where I come from, a coffee means a coffee and not something else
And a nightcap definitely means something else
And a break away together says something more
But over here in the land of the perpetual wet weekend
It just means we're going away, Have they no passion?
I've noticed the men here are inclined to lead you on
And then back off

Terrified of the consequences.
Well I'm pretty hot stuff you know!
Must be too cold- hearted, bless their cold wet socks.
Maybe my warm southern African blood
Makes me a creature of different habits.
Then where do you meet men?
Church – probably a bit boring
The pub – maybe not.
At work – definitely too close for comfort
Besides you're the weirdo that eats raw meat;
A friend of a friend?
Well, we're back to that communication problem again
So I'm thinking of starting a lonely hearts club
Maybe we can draw single people together
People who talk the same language
People who are vibrant and happy and in tune with their feelings
And not save their bright clothes just for summer,
Am I being too optimistic?
Is this a crazy thought?
Internet dating frightens me to death,
Not for me at all
They might like my appearance
But what happens when I open my mouth?
What happens when they discover I'm not one of them?
Perhaps it is my lot to be alone?
Perverts need not apply!

Yours
Lonely from Kingsbridge

I met him when I was seventeen

He was older
He was bolder
He snatched that balloon
I called my heart,
Cut the string,
And let it soar way up yonder.
Crushes I had aplenty,
But this one was different,
He was the first one to take notice,
To return the sentiment
And I was a goner,
My brain turned to mush,
Oh me, oh my
This dude was so lush!
I wanted him to be the one
I wanted him to step up,
And claim what was already his.
He said I was no baby
That I was a proper lady
Independent, intelligent and strong.
Surely he couldn't be wrong?
But my experience was limited
And if my true feelings were exhibited
I would have been eliminated;
My mother would never allow such a thing,
Any thought of it was prohibited.
But the deep and dark desire grew.
I saw forbidden images of us together
Every time I closed my eyes,

And I knew it would happen sooner or later.
So I dressed in my best
Told myself I was a grown up now
And a proper man was waiting for me.
Nervous was I
Hiding behind a cloud of perfume
And a shroud of innocence
Even though I portrayed an air of confidence,
And there he was
Waiting for me at the fountain
And he led me upstairs
On a merry dance
As I followed him down the garden path
The nectar of love is an addiction
Most sweet
And when I left him
I was a girl no more.
He was a delicious treat
My conquest was a great feat
For I had won a prize beyond compare
The risk had been worth the dare,
As for what they thought
What did I care?
He was mine
A guy so fine
And I held on to him for as long as I could.
Looking back on it now
I can only wonder how
He fell for a girl like me.
Our love lives in a place called the past.
We never talk of it,

Hidden in the dust of thirty years
But if you look at my son's eyes
The shape of his nose
The certain way he smiles
You will understand that his father's denials were only lies.
And although it could never be
He was once everything to me.
And would I have missed it,
If things could have been different?
No, not for a minute.

The butterfly in the room

Has landed on my hand
So beautiful and grand
I daren't move an inch
Or even flinch
For fear of frightening it away,
I can only sit and stare
Pretend I haven't got a care
I cannot show that I am captured
by the wonder of the moment,
Holding my breath
Afraid to exhale,
With half closed eyes
I bathe in its colourful splendour,
Iridescent and delicate
In a room full of moths,
I am filled with pride!
And cannot believe
He has chosen me.
I have never seen such a creature!
My heart is light
Gazing at this wondrous sight
And at this precise moment
Nothing else could possibly matter,
He is the Fascination
That fires my imagination,
My butterfly is like the love I feel
Unique in its simplicity
And yet so very real,
Oh beautiful thing,

Why have you decided to land on me?
Why have you singled me out?
I feel special
For I am made magnificent
By his presence,
Enriched by the experience
That can only happen
Once in a lifetime,
Then just as I think he will stay
And that it can last forever
Without any notice,
He up and flies away.
And all that remains
In my memory
Is how it felt
When for just one brief moment
The little butterfly was mine.

You stole into my thoughts today

As I went about my daily duties
And the memory of you sat very well with me
And so I willed you to come
Like ripples on river bed stones
I sent out waves on the conscious winds of connected minds
And by and by did you appear
Strolling in you sat for a while
And we spoke in whispers
And exchanged our secrets
The intimate repartee that close friends understand
And the little jokes and smiles and our shared conspiracies
Made my load lighter and the afternoon became brighter
And for a brief moment the sun appeared in at the window
And for a second I thought spring had come two months too early
Oh silent, secret friend
How the very thought of you
Brings gladness to my heart
I'm trying very hard not to be in love with you
I'm learning not to fall and just to appreciate the little moments
we share
I am hiding the fact that these very small things
Mean such a lot
So pleased am I that you find excuses
to see me
And it hasn't escaped my notice that you seek me out more now
that we no longer speak of that thing we must not talk about
And I shan't cross that line again.
So hold out your hand and this little bird will make a feast of
the crumbs

And when your smile draws me close
I will look away at anything
Other than your eyes
Lest I give myself away,
I will busy myself on some pointless task or other and not allow
myself to linger and melt under your gaze.
For if it must not be love
Then for goodness sake
Let it never be discovered
That these sentiments I feel
are real
And so I must be a traitor to my heart
And deceive the very person
I hold dearest
For rather give me a friendship than nothing at all.

Broken valentine

I chanced upon a musician
He walked in from the cold
Warmed his hands and started playing
Giving us a melancholy tune
The melody was soothing
His voice it was so sweet
He was young yet his style was classic
Timeless and astute,
The music, it flowed from his fingertips
like the breath within his chest
Naturally and flawlessly
It held us in its wake
I couldn't not help but wonder
From whence his talent came.
How could he know such music
His years had reached not that frame
And yet he played it as if he'd lived before
In a time he could not have belonged
In an era he could not have known.
At his age his songs should have been more modern
This man just passed thirty's turn
like someone far much older
Someone of my vintage
And how he introduced me to artists and things I'd never learnt
He stayed a while and tutored
I couldn't leave him be
There was a thing awakened
Deep inside of me
For what he gave I took

And kept and cherished
It was a rare gift
He left me and I thank him
With all the gratitude I possess.
But what he took
Cannot be replaced
For I am not human without it
Simply a mere husk
Missing that one component
That now belongs to him
He didn't really have a use for it
But it was all I had to give
And now that he has left us
I have no reason to live,
As for misery
I wallowed in it daily
Took to my verse
My devotion to him a curse
For my beautiful musician and I had to part
So off he went carrying my heart.

Can I help it?

I can't help it if I love your smile,
I can't help it that you've made my life worthwhile,
I can't help it if all I think about is you,
I can't help it if I skip down the avenue
With such a spring in my step,
And that I don't really fancy Johnny Depp
Coz he's not my type
Ain't no way!
Be my cream, be my Peach Melba
Coz I'd rather have Idris Elba!
Is it my fault that every time I see your eyes of brown
I act like such a clown
Pretending I don't care
When I wouldn't dare
Give anything away,
So careful with what I say,
Putting on a happy mood
When really you make me melancholy, Dude!
I wouldn't be so rude
To confess my undying devotion
In case it caused a commotion
And I wouldn't want to court disaster
Just because you make my heart beat faster
And I don't want you to stay away
And make me pine another day,
So I'll day dream
That someday I'll be your queen
And be the happiest girl you've ever seen,
Coz I can't help it that I'm crazy for you, honey,

And even though this feeling makes me feel funny,
It's also kinda nice.

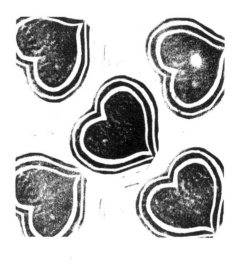

It's always this time of the year

When I think of you
Maybe it's the warm glow of the candle light
burning in the darkness of the night
That evokes your memory,
Or the thought that another year has passed us by;
I really believed that I'd laid your ghost to rest
I wrote the book
Told the story of you and I
Steadied my pen
Through the heartache and tears,
Purged my soul
Laid it open
For the world to see
What you had meant to me
I thought if I did this thing
I would be cured,
How wrong was I?
You will never leave me
My first love,
My only love.
The years go by
It's been such a long time,
And still I think of those days we shared
A half a lifetime ago,
The nights we slumbered together
Safe in each other's arms
Under the backdrop of a clear southern African sky
A vista of stars above us
When all our dreams were fused together

When all we had was that precise moment
That perfect summer
When the rain fell in abundance
Its life force breaking the drought
Bringing food and hope to our nation.
And between the showers
We walked in the vivid gardens
Breathing in the pure and revitalising air
In an Eden of our own.
Every day I woke up next to you
Was a gift, my darling.
I was under the illusion
That you loved me
And so young that I believed it would last forever.
Life has taken us very far from each other,
My dearest lover,
But my sentimental heart
Can't help but remember
That beautiful December
When you were all that I wanted
When I woke up on that Christmas morning.
I got my wish that year
Your love was mine
And I will always cherish that moment
And because I believe in miracles
I pray that one day
You will find your way
back to me.

I woke up this morning with sunshine in my heart

I woke up this morning with sunshine in my heart
(The weather was another story)
Valentine's Day at last!
Oh, the possibilities
Oh, the suspense
Does anyone fancy me?
Will I get a card?
Better still will I get a rose?
I wouldn't mind if he didn't declare himself
I rather like the mystery of a secret admirer
"To my darling
Be my Valentine
Love from X"
How romantic!!
How delicious
That would be bound to put a smile on my face
And keep people guessing all day long.
Red, that's what I'll wear
Red lipstick is always a must
I feel naked without it quite frankly;
I expel a cloud of perfume
And walk through the mist
Today is the day
Now is the hour
Perhaps a last-minute date
And an after-dinner mint left on my pillow
Oh, a girl must be prepared.
And then I remember

I do have a date and I mustn't be late
I'll set the alarm and be out of the door in time
An early morning rendezvous …
With the dentist!!
No choccies for me then
And I have a rather bad bout of sinus
I'll have to stay away from the roses too
Don't want to be sneezing,
No red lippy either
Can't get that on the dentist's equipment.
As reality bites
I head out the door into a shower of blinding winter rain
So, life isn't perfect
And love has decided to stay in the warm today.
To all those smug Valentines getting little surprises later
Enjoy the moment
Bask in the joy of feeling loved
You are the lucky ones!
For those of us having an un-Valentine's Day
Smile anyway
Love hasn't abandoned you
It just hasn't found you yet
So, go out and buy your own rose
Put it on your desk
Who cares
Nobody knows!!!
Wishing you hearts
roses and love,
Make it romantic whatever you do.

Oh, please be mine

Lover divine
And forever I will be thine,
These immortal words
Are inscribed in my heart.
For when I am in love
I'm consumed by it,
It is a raging, rising passion that fires desire
And ignites the world.
I once had a love
And I loved him well
How happy was I to gaze into his eyes,
How contented I was to be at his side
I would scoop him up in a warm embrace
And we would meld completely into one.
When I see photographs of my younger self
I see blissful happiness in my eyes,
In my smile,
I wanted him always
I wanted him forever
I treasured every minute in his company,
Every moment in his arms
And when we were fused together
I never wanted to let him go
To be a part of him, as he was a part of me,
Was my only wish.
When I learned to love him
I learned what the real essence of love was,
I yielded to his touch
Trusted his words

And gave myself to him completely
I saw that when we were together
The castle was strong
There was no force mightier than
The walls of our love
Even though an tempestuous storm of opposition, anger
and prejudice
Raged about us,
The space between he and I was a perfect space
The elements that made up his breath and mine were
indistinguishable
Because they were the same,
And colours that brightened our days
Had no monotones, no variations of the colour grey
Neither black nor white
We drove through a canopy of purple flowering trees
Watched birds of vivid yellow
And strolled through magnificent tropical gardens,
As if we'd stepped into an artist's water colour painting,
We attracted beauty
Because we were beautiful
And our love was pure
It was our time
His and mine
We spent it together like currency
we were given from some greater force;
And when all the precious sand had slipped into the bottom
of the hour glass
our time was up.
I was at first, very much aggrieved
By his going

But then, as time went on
I learned to smile again
And carried the memories we shared
with me,
They became a talisman
Their powerful magic helped me through
difficult times
And I realised the people we love
Don't go away
They are always there
Though we may only touch them in our dreams
Or in our poetry
They survive because we immortalise them,
Love did not fail
Or let us down
For if we had not experienced
It's joy, it's passion and how it made us feel
We would not be the people we are today,
And if perhaps in one coincidental moment
Our paths do happen to meet,
Across a room
Or in a crowded street
Those feelings we once shared
Would still be there
Of this there can be no doubt.
And so dear hearts,
I say to you
Never be blue if your true love
Says *adieu*
For love by its very nature
will return,

A fire needs to be fed to burn
And you will love again
In a different shape or guise
When you look into another's eyes,
For what you send out you will receive
So make your wish
And just believe.

Why do we always want what we cannot have?

So accessible, yet unobtainable
We watch from hooded eyes
Talking in riddles and rhymes,
Our brilliant disguise,
In our cleverly worded innuendos,
We hide the meaning of our desires.
It's all game of cat and mouse, you see,
That's how it goes with you and me,
You lean in, I lean away
You come close, I want to stay
But I cannot,
And so I fight the sentimental part of my heart
That turns to putty whenever you start,
And I pretend that I don't care
Nonchalantly, as if you're not there,
I look up, I see your eyes,
Sunshine and blue skies
Warming me from top to toe
Then I watch you as you go,
There's a full blown battle that's raging inside,
And even when you tease and chide,
I find it impossible to hide
And so I give it back with interest against my will
And even then I think of you still
The words, my responses, the false insults
We exchange,
They're really not real
And the total opposite to what I feel,

And so it's a war of will and wit
We don't mean anything, not one little bit,
A tiny sample of our exasperating banter
When to your side I'd gladly canter
But we must dance around in circles square,
And yet I find myself looking for you everywhere.
Oh come now,
Let's be fair,
Surely there's a part of you,
That wishes I were there,
If for nothing else
But to prove the golden rule,
That of us all, love makes a fool
And so I'd rather be a little jester
And leave this thing I feel to fester,
Even though the magnet's force
makes it impossible to resist,
Still I must desist,
For even though we are poles apart
Your very name is dear to my heart.

A perfect dream

Have you ever had one of those perfect dreams
Where everything is just right
And as it should be?
I found myself in that place a couple of evenings ago,
Walking down my driveway
In a garden I did not recognise
But knew to be my own,
And as I approached the gate
There you were,
Riding by on a bicycle,
It was a beautiful summer's day
The garden was green and fresh
In the morning air
And as I greeted you
I realised you were looking for my place,
As my future home was the second last house in the cul de sac,
The conversation between us was easy
As it flowed from one thing to the next,
The vibe was good,
I felt as light as the breeze
Even though you made some excuse
About helping a friend with a technical issue
When I asked what you were doing there,
I left you looking for the address
As I too leapt on my bike
Waving nonchalantly
floating down the street
My cotton dress billowing in my wake,
I was full of vim and vigour

Tanned as brown as bean
And strong.
The dream continued into other adventures,
I crossed a tiny bridge
A very strange contraption made of cogs and wheels
A beautiful feat of engineering.
I have no idea what the dream meant,
If anything,
But when I awoke the next morning
I felt revitalised, refreshed, replenished,
And realised that everything was going to be just fine,
Maybe we don't have all the answers for a reason
Perhaps this will be revealed in the fullness of time
Sometimes it's best not to know the future,
And for now we just have to be
And let things run its course.
So when you have that dream,
Enjoy it,
Let it wash over you,
And just bask in the glow for a while.
Hold on to anything that nurtures your spirit
Anything that feeds your soul.

Desire

Desire has spread through me
Like a hot savannah night
The density of the heat making me heady
With breathless purpose
And with a fervour I cannot escape,
An obsessive force,
Insatiable
Merciless,
I thirst for a gulp
From the delicious jug of love
To quench and drench
And cool these passions within,
I am woman
Strong
And yet defenceless
To resist
This temptation,
Primal
Instinctive
To pair two souls,
To find a mate,
Long and lonely is this night
Worn out am I from the fight
I cannot turn away
It pulls and pushes
Like a tidal wave building inside me,
I press my body against the wall
It's coolness gives some relief
From the fever on my skin,

I long to bathe
In tranquil waters
Under a dark sky
Meet you on the bank
In a secluded spot
Two shadows
Moving among the trees
Under the velvet cover of darkness
Intimate
Close
Familiar,
To breathe in the scent of you
Like an aphrodisiac
Mingling with the wild lilac
Carrying its perfume on the fragrances of the night,
Moonlight filtering through the leaves
Images of you captured
In my brain,
I push them out,
But back they come
And there they remain.
What is it about a summer's night
And its ability to over-excite
And feed this internal light
And the feeling I try to conceal,
What makes it so raw?
What makes it so real?
I cannot deny what I feel
Its buried too deep
Tucked away within,
I wouldn't know where to begin.

What if I found you at my door?

What If I found you at my door
One dark and mysterious night,
The secrets you hide behind your eyes
The smile that says you know what's passing between us,
Standing there leaning against the frame,
Fashionably aloof,
With just an undercurrent of sexual tension,
I feel the ebb and flow of my breath
realise I cannot control the rise and fall
Your silhouette on the wall,
My breasts rise
Exposing a little lace,
You glance down, suppressing a frown,
Then a grin breaks out;
Your very essence, your presence,
Strong yet subliminal,
Working on another level,
Firing off pheromones
That send the chemicals in my brain
on a collision course,
Like the bumper cars at the fair,
Your deep blue fragrance,
An aphrodisiac pushing this engine into overdrive.
It's been so long,
I'd forgotten what power
You wield,
Pure natural man,
We're close now
Breathlessness makes me heady

I feel the muscles of your arms
Through the thin shirt,
Desire is surfing the waves
Of my unsteady reason
Like a luxury yacht,
Untethered, bouncing on the surface of the water,
my defence systems are disabled
As assuredly as if the guards dogs were asleep beside the fire,
The white flag is hoisted
And flies above the turrets of the castle
The drawbridge is opened
I am ready to receive you,
Then, considering me from dark eyelashes
"Are we going inside then?"
My London bloke speaks
"It's brass monkeys out here!"

He took my hand

He took my hand and held it,
Just for a short while,
A tiny little moment of heaven
A fleeting pleasure,
So unexpected,
And yet the very sensation of it
Carried me off
And kept me floating away on a glorious soft cloud,
And so it happens time and time again
Whenever it comes sneaking back
Into my memory,
A welcome intruder,
A little friend,
How comforting it feels.
I see us sometimes ,
your hand in mine,
Childlike in our simplicity,
As our fingers meet and intertwine
Your skin, my skin
One entity.
A prayer, a whisper, a little encounter
Between two,
How snug it feels
Palm to palm
Spiritual, yet sensual,
Smooth yet tender,
Like lighting a candle in a dark, sacred space,
Uniting your body with mine
A little intimacy,

Nothing really,
Reaching out for someone,
Reaching out for you,
Borrowed for a time,
And yet I know your hand
Like the back of my own
The softness, the tone,
It thrills me to the bone,
An invisible chord that has attached itself to my heart.
We touch so many things in our lives,
But that one touch from someone special
Awakens the senses
Ignites the soul
Holding on,
Not tightly, just loosely comfortable,
The briefest of interludes,
A shared experience
Mutually given, willingly received
And then retrieved,
Taken back,
letting go, slipping from the clasp
Falling away from our grasp,
And for a while the energy lingers
In the space
Our hands have held,
And then it vanished
Like it was never there.

Slow dancing to Tina Turner

I had a flashback today
To a time when we were
Slow dancing to Tina Turner,
All alone in your flat in Avondale
When I had run away from him
To spend a few precious, stolen moments with you
We were swaying to the music
Two people
Together, alone, lost and found
Content and tormented,
And my heart was magnetised to yours
Completely joined together
And neither of us wanted anything else
But that moment
Nothing
Not even a breath
Could separate us
Because we were one breath
One heartbeat.
My memory of that day
is as clear today
As when it happened
And I as sit here some twenty five years later
And remember
The feel of your body
Having you in my arms
The sweet harmony that surrounded us
In the falling light of the early evening
Knowing that soon I would have to leave you,

I couldn't have loved you any more if I tried
It saddens my heart to think of what could have been
And it makes me wonder
What will the soul remember
When you and I are no longer here?
I'd like to think you'll look for me
When we pass into eternity
For nothing could have been closer to heaven
Than that moment
When you danced with me.

If kisses were wishes

If in some dream you come to me
How joyous I would be
For dreams are a manifestation of our reality,
And so when we lay down and drift off
Fantastic fantasies take flight
And all the things that bind
Us to these earthly cares
Are cut
As we soar ever upwards.
Last night saw us together
in my dream,
Even though that is only a wish,
I called you over for a kiss
Our lips meet
Like some buttery tasting sweet
And oh how I wanted to linger a little longer,
You told me not to be greedy,
But one sweet is never enough for me,
And so I asked for one more
Even though you made light of my request
You little tease,
I noticed you didn't resist
And so we shared another delicious moment
Our friends looking on bemused,
Witnessing the temporary binding of two souls,
For what else is a kiss
But a vapour of mist
Shared when two auras infuse,
And my dear,

Though your kisses were few
I savoured each one
And keep them in my butter cookie jar,
For each was a blissful delight
Each was an unexpected surprise,
That took me to a higher height
The moment my heart did a merry skip,
For one scrumptious sip
Of that sweet summer wine
With you and I frozen in time.

Passion is ...

Passion is a red hot Latin lover,
A night with Idris Elba,
Jennifer Lopez's beautiful eyes,
The promises and lies
We tell our beating hearts,
Wearing rouge allure lipstick
Chanel No. 5,
The things that keep us alive,
Red roses on a dark wood piano
And the edge of the garden where the wild flowers grow,
Flamenco dancing on a hot Spanish night
Dreaming of Mr Right,
English mid-summer strawberries
Ripe, juicy and ready,
Like your lips
The night we kissed;
Foreign holidays,
Crossing the water on long distant ferries,
That pretty black dress
Transforming you into a princess
When you feel like a mess;
Loving someone when you know it's hopeless,
Hiding behind a smile
When you're dying inside
But going along for the ride,
None-the-less,
A friendship that could have been more
If you hadn't stopped to adore,
Passion is a blessing

Passion is a curse
In a world that's adverse
To great shows of affection
The norm seems to be rejection.
Well, I've never been mediocre
I'd rather be livin' *la vida loca*
So be who you are
At your crazy passionate best
Don't worry about the others
You're living life
And you are truly blessed.
To heck with all the rest!

An ordinary Friday

It was just an ordinary Friday afternoon
The week could not go by too soon,
With all its worries and stresses
Sitting heavy on my shoulders,
…When suddenly
Out the corner of my eye,
A vision of extraordinary loveliness see I,
Descending a ladder,
From the heavens above,
He flipped my world on its axis,
This beautiful apparition,
Where the heck has he been hiding all my life?
His shoulders, his legs
Carrying that load of tiles
Muscles, sweat, skin
Come on, I'm only human!
He smiled and waved,
This cheeky chap
Was that a wink?
I've got to know his name!
Like a moth to a consuming flame
Here I go again!!
And I have to say
I am enjoying the view!
He blocks my way with a piece of wood
Was that deliberate, I wonder,
Too breathless to move,
I'm scuppered well and good
I'll have to wait now,

An apologetic look
Shy, engaging,
Something hidden behind those beautiful dark eyes,
Attraction instant
Will he make the first move?
Oh my goodness
Will you leave the man alone
He's got a job to do!
I walk passed again
He gives me the eye,
I cannot deny
I'm feeling pretty high,
His mates tease from above
Got to get his number
He looks just like Idris Elba!
Get a grip girl,
Get your mind off what you're thinking right now!
So off I drift off on my flights of fancy
And oh do I fancy the pants off him!!
And now that ordinary Friday
Has turned into something completely magnificent
And the smile on my face
Is not easy to disguise.

Oh, my far and distant love

Stop pulling at my heart strings
Why wound your little white dove?
Every time I think of you, my aching soul sings
Although I'm wretched over the love of you,
Oh my dearest, why do you make me so blue?
How much longer will this heart of mine
Bleed and pine
Over this old love of thine,
Who didn't give a toss
About the loss
Of me
Although to my heart, he held the key
For my devotion didn't mean as much to him as it did to me,
Why am I drawn to such?
When will I learn
And no more yearn
For the love of an ice-cold heart?
I knew it from the start
But when I thought I might win
I started to begin
To think it would last
And love came thick and fast
And passion burned strong
And I felt we would always belong
Side by side
With love as our guide,
And for a while you remained
But now my face is tear-stained
As although my love was true

It was not the same for you.
The flame still burns bright
Here in my bleakest night
But when I think all hope as taken flight
In my heart there is a light
That I feel will never fade
Although goodbye is what you bade
And so I am doomed to sigh
For I will love you till I die,
Oh cruel heart, I am a hopeless case
With melancholy written on my face
And I'll love you from a distance,
In spite of your inconsistency,
And perhaps some day
You might say
That you cared for me just a little
Even though you were non-committal.
And all my hopes will not be in vain
For on my door you might knock again.

In Avonlea did I lay my head

Next to yours and so to dream
As lovers do
Side by side
Entwined with you.
And the jasmine was particularly beautifully scented that year
As beside the open window
We slept
With stars for our fairy lights
And the moon swooned into your room.
And I floated around on a cloud full of daisies
And my eyes saw nothing but the love I had for you
And you complained about my cooking
And made us pots of *sadza* to eat
With green vegetables
And bully beef
Because the budget was tight
But nobody minded
and we had steak on payday,
As we sat on the veranda and shared Lion lager
And I took puffs of your Kingsgate cigarettes
Even though you said I could have one of my own,
I liked to put my lips
Where yours had been,
It felt like we were kissing again,
And I polished the parquet flooring
On hands and knees
Because I wanted your house
To look beautiful,
And you tended to the roses

While I watched you from the kitchen
I loved to see you work
Muscles tight and gleaming from your exertions
And the weather was warm and balmy
And yellow weaver birds made upside down nests
And when the drought broke we danced in the rain
And you called me crazy
Because I washed my hair in the gutter pipe,
And we loved and laughed
And made love every night
And on lazy afternoons;
My workmates shook their heads at the love-bites
And my boss turned a blind eye,
And we made out in the park
In front of the Monomotapa Hotel in the shadows of the trees,
And life was good
And we were happy
That idyllic summer we spent together.

We met after an absence of ten or so years

It might have been more
Who can say?
A spontaneous decision to meet at Oliver Tambo Airport.
I, on my homeward flight back to my life in England
And for you a little respite
From yours in Johannesburg,
You walked toward me
In that crowded space
People looking on,
And you held your arms open wide
And I went into the place
Where I once belonged
Where I will always belong,
The melding of our two souls
Once more
My true North
My plane of perfection
Close to you,
And for a few brief seconds
Our poles were aligned
And all the pressure and complications of our lives dissipated
My spirit floated into yours lighter than a feather
A kiss and then we parted our bodies,
Animated in our conversation
Warmly wrapped in each other's company
And we wandered into the busy restaurant
And chatted about our families
You confessed some secrets I never knew,
You asked about our son,

And for a moment we remembered
How we once began,
We smiled and there was no distance,
And the passage of time meant nothing because it was exactly as
it always was,
How we always were with each other
I wanted the afternoon to last forever,
I would have traded everything to have stayed there with you,
I don't remember what we ate,
Or how quickly the hours passed
Because I was swimming in your deep, dark eyes,
I was leaning into you completely,
And you took my hand and held it
And I remembered how it always fitted perfectly into yours,
The force of attraction between us
Tender yet strong
Had not diminished,
I remembered how we once held each other,
Our naked bodies reflected in a mirror on your wall
And I wanted to go back there,
At once.
I wanted to rewind the clock,
Stop it completely
But our time was up soon enough
And so in the lift we spent, one more precious moment
And you pulled me close
As down it went,
And I felt that surging breathlessness I always felt
Whenever you were near,
We made a joke about the biscuits being crushed
To deflect from the inevitable

Because we knew we would soon be parting,
And so on to the departures gate
And one final embrace,
And the last kiss lingering and sweet
Yet it was years since we had been lovers,
And the goodbye...
I saw you through the glass
Walking away,
And the rain on the aircraft windows
Competed with the tears that ran down my cheeks.

It started with a song

It started with a song
You played,
How I fell asleep with your voice in my ear,
Holding my transistor close
And how you seeped into my bones,
How our romance blossomed
Over the airwaves,
My last year of school
My famous boyfriend,
A secret we kept to ourselves,
My first crush,
And by the time it had grown into something deeper
I was hopelessly in love and utterly surrendered to all your charms,
The meaning of the music intensified,
Our heart beats mingled with the melody
The lyrics spoke of our deepest desires,
And then the impossible happened ...
The deejay became mine
And I couldn't believe that I held the dream in my hands,
You were tumbling, stumbling and falling too,
And that all the tunes were dedicated to me.
When did that happen?
How did that happen?
My poor defenceless heart,
The way you walked,
The smoke rings you blew into the air,
And the other girls' stares,
and I felt invincible
Walking by your side,

I remember how we danced,
Close, one entity;
And when we were together,
I felt I belonged to no one
Other than you,
And they all knew that I was your girl,
Unschooled in the ways of love,
I believed the songs,
I thought it would last forever,
Impressionable, young and completely naive
I was consumed by the fire
The passion
The everlasting desire,
You took me and made me your lifelong slave,
For I am lost without you,
My dearest darling,
Your love set the bar,
I found everything I needed
When I was seventeen
No one has even come close,
What hope is there for me?
The vibe we shared took me to that place deep inside,
The place I call home.
And now you're gone
Far away in the past
And yet the memory of you lingers,
into the darkness of another
Long and lonely night,
And as the love songs play
I close my eyes and sway
Remembering yesterday.

Looking for my Mr Darcy

Today I went to Bath
Hopping on board the train,
Totnes station colourful and interesting
Music playing in my ears
In tune with my happy heart
Arriving on time and looking my best
I trawled the streets
Frosty was the wait
Busy were the pavements,
I checked my mobile
Delayed
Some hold up on the motorway
outside Coventry,
I was optimistic
So up and down I wandered
Keeping warm
Watching the lovers, the parents and friends
Arrivals and departures
Waiting for Mr D
Another text
Still stuck
I went in search of something warm
Caffè Nero beckoned
Hot chocolate and a slice of carrot cake
On to the street again
Aching feet
Fraying slightly at the edges
Not a sign of the elusive man
Busy shops

Jostling through the crowd
Children, prams, couples
I passed the Roman Baths
Gift shop carefully avoided
On I went
Leaden legs
Into the Jane Austen Centre
He was nowhere to be seen
Did I want a t-shirt?
"I love Mr Darcy"
Frankly I've gone off him!!
He's a work of fiction
Safely tucked away in a dusty tome
I will not dream of him in that wet shirt
Nor will I pretend to be Elizabeth Bennett
Another text
Turning back, too late
Oh well, so am I
"The train to Totnes is delayed by 45 minutes"
Oh what torture
Don't think my feet will get me to platform 2.
I went in search of Mr Darcy today
But all I got was blisters for my trouble
It is a truth universally acknowledged
Mr Darcy doesn't exist!

For it is written

Nobody loved you like I did,
There have been others
Before and since
Who have held my fascination
Grabbed my attention
But not like you,
I thought you were my missing half,
The utmost, innermost, the only one
I could ever imagined
Walking by my side,
You dwell in my heart
In my psyche
In my blood,
Old souls are we
The black to my white
The yin to my yang
For there can be no light without the darkness
And I've spent my happiest moments
In the dark with you,
And my most content
Sleeping in the soft dawn light
In the crook of your arm;
Passion that passed between us
Flowed like melted butter
Wrapping us both in a warm glow
You gave me that rush,
Made me breathless
When you looked at me
Touched me,

I knew you were meant for me
I recognised that from the first time I heard your voice
Held your hand
We just fitted together,
Defied the odds, the opposition and the obstacles
And if you walked through that door now
Today,
At this very moment,
Even after everything that has passed
All the pain
The splintering of a broken heart
The years apart
I would not turn you away
How could I ?
Please tell me that in all honesty?
This is something that transcends space and time
And I'd feel the same 1000 years from now
In another dimension,
Another moment in time
In a different constellation,
For once the flame is lit
It continues to burn
In the cave,
In the furthermost nave
In this life or the next
In stone was carved this text
I am yours
And yours alone.

He slipped into my life when I wasn't looking

Suddenly there he was,
I wasn't looking for love
And he wasn't really offering
He wasn't even asking
And we weren't dating
And yet there I was waiting,
For my support, shoulder, friend
to appear.
A glint of sunshine on the window pane,
Light at the end of a dark lane,
Not there, always there
Non-relationship relationship,
The person who dropped everything
To come to my aid
Who seeks me out like a missing twin
So does it need a label?
Do we need to analyse
What's happening here?
I drink sweet wine
Taste it on my lips
like the kisses I long to steal
The beautiful hands I long to feel.
He drinks his tea strong, this Yorkshire lad
Teabag left in the cup.
Refuses the wine I offer.
It is dark red
Like the passionate feelings
That rise and subside

Deep inside,
I confess, I confide
Laying side by side, we hide
As I dance around the words
he honestly finds
necessary to express
to my begging heart,
Lest the meaning be misconstrued
it is blindingly clear,
My beloved one,
Hope that is building
Must not
For you have told me it can never be
Your heart belongs elsewhere,
Far away across the sea
There's nothing,
Not even a crumb, left for me.
The comfort and ease builds between us
It lingers,
And like a hand that beckons
It draws us so close
There isn't a breath between us,
And yet we must not touch
Nor caress at my door
A kiss is not allowed
Yet I am filled with contentment,
I let you go without dread
For when we are apart this non-existent romance
Plays out in my head.
It breaths,
it is alive

Watered by hope of what has not been promised.
In my eyes you are ever there
Your absent presence holds me firm
It orbits around me
Your smile,
Your little chuckles,
Be you near or miles afar
No matter,
I feel it.
If some time, my love,
your heart stumbles and falls into my grasp
I will hold it tightly
Never let it go.
It is a prize worth having.
This is something I believe to be so
The hour may be late
But this precious thing is worth the wait.
So the tears I cry are mine alone
The longing that lurks in the dark is my secret weakness.
As the mist throws a blanket on the estuary bed
And the night begins anew
The wind that blows across Bowcombe Bridge
Will find its way to you too.
So I send it with my love and stand aside
As the water brings loneliness in on the tide
And I turn in once again
and try to hide the pain
As my tears fall like sweet, warm rain.

Reminisces of a quixotic soul

It suddenly occurred to me in the late hours of the night
That tonight would be that night
That I would finally get it right
So I took out my pen
steadied my hand
And I started to put down the reasons
Why I have this feeling that just won't shift
It is often in the deep dark hours
That the answers become so clear
When daylight concerns with convention, ties our thoughts up
in knots
And we can't speak what we feel
Hiding our innermost desires away
For fear of reprisal, rejection, repercussion,
It's good to retreat into those places
And just observe the authentic self
No need to wear the daily mask
No need to hide under a film of make-up
To conceal the blemishes
For I tonight am alone with myself
And I think for what it's worth
I'm doing okay
So I haven't got a million pounds in the bank
I might not have Beyoncé's looks
And I haven't sold fifty thousand books,
But I have an imagination that runs in riotous abandon
And although my romances are mainly in my head
What does it matter?
Who cares that I listen to the same some song five hundred times,

And that it always reminds me of you?
It is this self-indulgent madness that keeps me sane.
But I at least I have the ability to fall
Head over heels in love
imaginary lovers or not
This is my reality
I'm content to be here
Don't reach in and pull me out
For I would be unutterably miserable in the real world.
I want to believe love is a beautiful, breathing thing
I won't give up hope that the perfect mate is out there
And some day if I'm very lucky
He will find me.

It was just one afternoon a long time ago

It shouldn't have happened
But it did,
I take full responsibility
For that moment of passion
Up in the rafters
Between the sheets
in my lover's bedroom
Although it was you who asked him for the key
It was I who instigated it,
He didn't know it was me you were meeting there
Neither did she, your significant other
I doubt she ever did, you were the perfect mate
Cared and loved her till the end.
And as for the other person we deceived,
Well, he probably deserved it,
Not as if he ever appreciated what he had
Otherwise I wouldn't have gone looking for it
In the arms of another,
What you wanted to give me I needed so desperately,
So we'll call that a debt paid.
It took a lot of pursuing, a lot of persuasion
I didn't think you'd ever weaken
You were so strong
So resolute to my "come ons" even though I had known you forever
The chase took twelve months
Every minute delicious torture
Perhaps it had been lurking longer
And even I hadn't been aware of the growing desire,
Those evenings on the veranda

While she packed up, we smoked, chatted, flirted
I, trying to give you the signals.
Said she'd see you at home
Drove off
Left us to talk.
Oh my, your eyes left me utterly defenceless
The breathing shallow in my chest
How did I ever manage to construct a coherent sentence?
I drank you in, took your image with me when you left
Replayed it when I turned away from him to sleep.
Skin as smooth as *mukwa*,
Strong, handsome, so easy to fall for
And I felt myself rolling and tumbling
I couldn't let it go
I had to have you
I didn't realise you felt the same
But you were too honourable, too good,
Then it happened... I couldn't believe it
And so it was
We met in secret
Stole away from our lives and complications
To make love up in the dappled shadows
Reflections of sunlight coming through the skylight window
Just for a few hours
This is how friendship moved up a notch
And how the two of us waded into forbidden waters
For a few brief hours
Everything was suspended
Nothing existed except what we were doing
It couldn't happen again
We knew that

Which made it even more special.
And when it was over we locked it away.
Hid the key deep in our hearts.
I wonder if they'd ever guess the secret behind our eyes?
And how when we met later
I'd be able to hide
The bashful glances I'd steal at you
Or would they catch you gazing at me
Through some lull in the conversation?
Would we see ourselves as we were that day,
Remembering the twisted sheets
And our perspiration, ecstasy and pain of having to turn away?
The taste of your salty skin
The urgency of your kisses
The way you brushed my hair afterwards
Slow and gently
With such tenderness.
One delicious taste
An agreement between us two
... just one time.
A salve to cure the passion we could not deny
Is it wrong to allow yourself one single slip
In a life of blameless perfection?
And is it worse not to admit it took place?
If no one knew it happened
How can it do any damage?
It's so long ago now
Nothing remains of that day except the feeling that rises from
the pit of my belly every time I think of it.

I wonder if he likes strawberry jam?

It was the eyes that caught me by surprise
Two arresting placid blue light catchers
Deep, unfathomable, completely alluring, like a welcoming soft
afternoon haze.
I could not help but fall right into those azure pools
As I struggled to swim to the surface
Of my calm centre.
It was too late of course; the damage was done.
So, I put up the white flag and went jumping right into their
depths
It wasn't difficult once I'd leapt over the edge
They were hypnotic, mesmeric.
Then he reached right in and grabbed hold of my heart.
Every time I see him, he holds it in his hands.
Tosses it up like a ball
It follows him everywhere
Running here and there.
When he walks out of the room
It leaves with him
And when he's gone
The emptiness cannot be measured.
It sits on top of me like bag of spuds
Weighting me to the spot.
Yet my imagination runs away on
Flights of fantastical wonder
And when he sang that Dylan song
It was then that I released I was too far gone.
The evocative pictures were already painted in my head,
The two of us side by side on that big brass bed,

He, on the guitar, and I slowly melting away under a
coverlet of white.
The seduction was complete.
His voice would make angels weep.
And so, I imagine the touch of his hand on
the inside of my thigh
I see his arms around my waist.
But those lips, my oh my!
I'd like to tie him to chair
Side astride his lap,
Two silk scarves and a jar of something sweet.
Then I'd lick, kiss and tease
That soft mattress of red
His mouth is so fine, so full
I long to taste its delight... damn!
I wonder if he likes strawberry jam?

On reflection

On reflection you were bloody marvellous
So, you didn't look twice at me
What the heck?
You looked once that's all that counts
And you did linger for a while
And we did have fun while it lasted
And your kisses left the sweetest taste
And even now I smile when I think of them
And when I see you my heart still leaps
At the sight of you
So what, if the feeling wasn't mutual, it meant something to me
And I guess it always will
And the memory sits easy with me
The time we spent together was the most pleasant of interludes
In this humdrum thing we call life,
And if they catch me staring into space
Over the rim of my coffee cup
It's because I'm thinking of you,
Or whilst contemplating the rain drops out of the office window
I'm reminded of something that passed between us.
Some people possess that infinite gift
the ability to spread joy wherever they go,
It's not meant to be possessed
It's not meant to be kept
It's only fleeting
A sparkly thing
Brought out on special occasions
And oh, how it lifts the spirits
How the butterflies escape whenever I try to keep them in

And if they wonder why I'm smiling
Well they'll never guess the reason
Because I only know
That you were mine
For just one summer season.

An exercise in irony

I don't love you
 Really, I don't
And I didn't send it, or even write that note.
And there's absolutely no space in my heart
Not even one small part
Not a corner tucked away
That I can honestly say
Belongs to you.
And you never make feel blue
With the things you don't do
Because I'm as happy as Larry
Yes, I am, Pally.
And I don't go to sleep with your name on my lips.
And my heartbeat never skips
When you walk by,
And you've never once made me cry
As for my dreams you'll never be a part of those.
And the poetry and prose
I wouldn't waste my lines
On two hearts that will never bind,
I haven't got the time
For that would surely be a crime
To ponder and pine
Whither and whine
For someone who will never be mine.
I never think of you, not at all
Not in summer, spring or fall
Not first thing in the morning
As the day is dawning,

Nor at night
When stars are shining bright
Or when the moonlight ripples through.
No, I wouldn't dare think of you.
And when I sit staring into space
Don't think for one minute I'm thinking of your face.
I never wonder what we'd do on a pleasant evening
When I'm busy looking at the ceiling.
I never imagine intimate seaside suppers
Or making you strong hot cuppas
Or walks hand in hand
Discovering foreign lands,
Woods full of blue bell blooms
Or snuggling up in sultry rooms
Riding off into the sunset on camels' backs
Or choosing colourful carpets on market racks.
No, I don't think of you, not that often
And if on occasion you do sneak into my thoughts
It's probably because I'm out of sorts.
I'm not ill in that sense,
Certainly not now in the present tense
maybe I was in the past
Inflicted by a malaise but it didn't last
And if I did at one time think fondly of you
And wonder and hope if love was true
This not now the case
In fact, I've given up the chase
And step away with grace.
For I will not fret
If you forget
My smile, my number or to call

So please don't mention it at all.
And if you listen to rumours you might hear
And think that I might hold you dear
Because of something I might have said
Or some poem I wrote that you've read,
Please don't take it to be true
And think that I love you.
For why would I set out to deceive
And give you something I could never retrieve?

The dangerous addictive nature of dark chocolate

I saw him from across the room
Looking at me with those "come and get me" eyes.
70% dark cocoa
I could just leap up and drop into those pools of temptation.
Best leave well alone!
He'd have me under his duvet before I could say mochaccino
Absolutely not,
you're an absolute no-no!
And yet I am magnetically drawn to your corner of the café,
That blue silk shirt clinging to your half-exposed chest
It's too much for a girl to resist.
Lashes of ebony, framing hooded eyes, surveying the territory
With a cool sartorial grace
That chiselled face, those tight white chinos.
Get away from my imagination
Go away from my thoughts
Not tonight Gino,
Not this week
Not ever!!
He calls me over
I'm hypnotised
I follow his gaze
"So, girl, you free?"
Who me?
I giggle
Can't you see I'm working?
"I'll have another. Make it a long one."
I pour the strong macchiato

Think of those long fingers
Milk?
"I like a little"
I bet you do!
He picks up the paper
Thumbs through l'Opinion
So, he understands French!
He's so sophisticated
He opens his cigarette case
Takes out a Cuban cigar.
Blue lips, blue smoke as he lights up.
Up he gets and walks towards the door
I make my move
I block the doorway
"You haven't paid."
"It's on the table." He smiles.
I step aside
He walks down the street.
I go to clear the cup.
The money and a note.
"I would have stayed ... if you'd have asked, *Cherie*"
And a piece of bitter, dark chocolate.
I open it
It dissolves on my tongue.
I'm about to throw away the wrapper
I see a telephone number and 7pm tonight,
Scrawled in a slanting script.

Naughty little Cupid

Alas he loved me not
But I haven't forgotten
My half- closed eyes
And the taste of that butterscotch softness of his lips.
Though his kisses were few
I remember them all
For they were so unexpected
Took me by surprise every time,
And the way that block of butter melted in the pit of my belly
When he called me "Love,"
The way he wore his cap,
His cheeky grin, holding my hand as we ran into the dark
Leaving them all wondering.
I loved every delicious drop,
Planned adventures,
Plotted conspiracies,
The incredible intimacy of our conversations,
That kept everyone guessing.
The places he showed me
The moments we shared
 Were all such treats
I got carried away in the rose-tinted haze
Drowning completely in his laughter
Falling utterly under that spell
And the magic and excitement of the moment
When I believed it might just happen.
Silly, hopeless romantic heart,
How could you lead me so wrongly down a path that took me to
the edge of a dream

And then shook me awake to the cold reality of morning?
Love beckoned me follow and merrily I skipped along,
For who am I to resist such a playful imp?
Honest to goodness, I really ought to know better at my age,
But this fella, made me forget all that
And I felt a mere girl with all the exuberance of youth,
at the first flush,
Which just goes to prove
There's nothing quite like the feeling
And why they call it falling
But to me it felt more like soaring
For I was higher than the clouds.
Oh Love, you fickle friend,
Why have I gone and done it all over again?

The couple at the end of the jetty

I saw the couple at the end of the jetty
looking out over the water
On one of those unexpected days in winter
When you would almost believe it was spring
A day between Christmas and New Year
Families out walking their dogs
Children riding new bicycles and scooters given as presents.
And as the man and woman stood there buttoned up against the
chilly wind
The weak sunshine showed a shy smile
Behind white clouds
Their togetherness completely separate
from the activities going on around them;
I envied them
Taking this time together
And I, an onlooker from the window of the train
As the boats lay devoid of people in the harbour
A row of little teeth in an empty mouth along the shore
And the children called out to their mothers
And fathers chased after them fearful of them riding off the path
and into danger;
I spotted a lone fisherman on the mud flats
Catching his tea
And the egret poking about in the slosh
The letters in the wall spelling out "Teignmouth", flashed passed
and I knew I was close to home
And the sea gave way to an estuary and that to the river
And soon we were by the siding and then the Totnes station
The train was late arriving

Sixteen minutes to be precise
Which is more than I can say for the Cross Country Train service
Who are hardly ever precise
And as I alighted, I thought of the couple
Would they have a fish and chip supper in a nearby pub?
Were they saying a fond goodbye after spending Christmas together,
Or were they just beginning?
Perhaps they always did this every year?
It's hard to predict just what, if anything at all was exchanged
out there
I was the silent observer who they would never know
And could hardly suspect they even had a witness
to that very tender and private moment beside the sea.

Love knows

Do not look at love with cynical eyes
We have all known the blissful innocence of first love
That breathless elation
That carried us off on a cloud of perfect happiness,
Weightless
Carefree
Do you remember a time
When you were happy to just be alive?
Untethered,
The string cut lose,
Floating
Dreaming,
The longing
The not knowing
The drama of the suspense
The secret of your desire
Not telling
Keeping your feelings hidden
And yet smiling outwards
And inwardly
Because they did not know
What you did!
That pure release,
When your heart flew away
On the breeze
When love came seeping into your pores
Breaking all the laws
Of reason
Of logic

Your parents' scorn,
The sweet elixir
Ambrosia you tasted
With that first kiss
And the memory of it
That washes over you even now
Even though the years have gone by,
And the ghost of that old love
Creeps up on you
Every once in a while
And taps you on the shoulder
Reminding you
that it was all worthwhile.

Love gone wrong song

I want to write a love song
Not to show that I'm clever
Or smart
But to show the world
How you once owned my heart.
You went and showed me something akin to heaven
Gave me new experiences
And pleasures aplenty,
Walked me into a dream
I've never known anything like it
Although one or two have come close
But nothing like
Your heart and mine
When love and destiny combine
And two spirits entwine
And now I find I'm lost in that time
But how, Dear Love,
Do I put this to music
In the lyrics of a song?
Come find me
Lead me back into yesterday
Take my hand and remember
When with love filled eyes
You looked at me
Took the breath from me,
Reached in and captured me completely
There you sit a million miles
Removed from those heady days
Of love newly discovered,

We type emails,
Avoid the subject
Of how you moved on
Walked away from me
Leaving me with my heart
Overflowing with love.
Everyone likes happy endings
And they would soon tire
Of me and my song
And how it all went wrong.

The other brother

The other brother was never my lover
Even though he once
Showed me a house
Proposed,
Offered me his heart
But you already had mine right from the start
And the other brother was the wrong one,
And so it was with you that I went,
And when you painted the town red
The other brother kept me company
"Let's go out," he said
The other brother was a bit wild,
The youngest child,
But with me he was always meek and mild
You were charming
Where he was practical
Sensible
Stable
Supportive
He gave me honesty,
You said the right things
Stole candy from the baby,
He did the right things,
Always treated me like a lady,
But he never knew
The you I saw.
The other brother warned me about your faults
Said he had his doubts,
I said I would find out for myself

But the die, you see, was cast,
I closed my eyes
And hoped it would last,
But that's all in the past,
No longer do I look at you
With naive eyes,
When we strip back all the deception and lies,
I don't think I owe you any loyalty,
But can I cross that line
When once upon a time
You were mine?
The years have gone by
And our boy has a boy of his own
Not that you would have known
For all the interest you have shown,
And now as we face the autumn of our years
And I no longer have any fears
Is it possible I can reverse the tears
And find contentment
Elsewhere?
Could the other brother and I become a pair?
Do you think that its fair,
To give him something you rejected
Something you neglected,
When he is standing there with open arms?

His song

His song calls to me
From a distant land
Across the sea,
The land where I was born;
The melody filtrates
In undulating tones
Across deserts
Rivers,
Breaking barriers,
Different time zones
And I am completely immersed
In still waters of calm,
His voice turns back closed pages of my heart
Urging me forth on a willing journey to the start,
The beginning,
The middle,
The end,
And even in the subdued light of a northern morning
I am comforted by its tenderness,
As if he were with me
in this room
At this precise moment,
And in my mind's eye
I see him sitting here
Strumming his guitar
with eyes closed
Feeling the music infiltrating his soul,
Saturating mine
With love for this man,

The warmth of our first cup of coffee
Our first morning kiss,
The image soothes my longing soul
The tranquillity after the storms of life,
Like the magnitude of an embrace,
It offers respite
To a weary mind
To the giver and the receiver,
A journey's end,
A brand new beginning
A place to bide for a while,
Green shoots,
The promise of spring
After a long, cold winter,
A moment for two spirits to wander
Unhindered by distance and time
What a rare and precious gift
This beautifully crafted song,
A little insight into a kindred spirit's heart,
A kindred spirit's soul.

She

She looks for me in the silence of the small hours
When she slips into my bed
And spoons into the small of my back
Wanting to share my warmth,
And sometimes she allows me to sleep in
And other times she awakes me from my dreams
With a soft touch on my face,
She doesn't ask for much
Except my full attention,
And she likes her breakfast on time
And often wants to share mine,
She can be quite indifferent at times
And doesn't want any frills
But lets me pay the bills,
And allows me to share her space,
She doesn't mind my music
Or listening to the same song a hundred times over,
She quite likes the telly
But flatly refuses to let me get lost in a book
And nudges my hand until I put it down,
She's not keen on mobile phones
And will often push it away
Or invade the space between the device and my head
Social media is wasting her time, she's often said,
She's content to sit beside me
Wants me to herself
Or very often she perches on my lap
Whatever affection dictates,
She prefers to be closer

Likes to hear the beating of my heart,
She doesn't like it if I'm late
And often tells me off,
And if I go away
She sulks for days,
Gets an upset tummy,
She likes our quiet little ways,
But when the moon is high in the sky
She departs without saying goodbye
And drives me near frantic
With her antics
As I wait and wonder and worry
At where she has got to,
And then when I'm sleep-worn and anxious
And I can't take it anymore,
She returns
Flops down and can't understand why I've been so pedantic
And falls asleep for hours,
Totally oblivious to my woes,
Sometimes she brings back presents
To say she's sorry,
Of these, I am not keen
Fresh from the kill
Or still alive
She toys with them for ages
And then she feels the rough edge of my tongue
Although she takes no notice,
We've had long conversations about the rights and wrong of the thing,
She gives me her looks and her silence,
And I know I've lost the argument,
But she's hopelessly devoted

When I'm poorly,
And never leaves my side,
Checks to see if I'm breathing from time to time,
She wants to know I'm still alive
And when I'm starting to revive
She cuddles in beside me
And softly starts to purr,
She keeps me going
I do it all for her,
For she's the mistress of this house,
And some days when this world seems a lonely place,
I only have to see her face
and then I feel happy, you see,
For she's chosen me.

If ever I marry again

If ever I marry again, it will be in May
When each day is as special as the last
Beauty breaking out in passionate desperation
To give the finest show,
Lilac blossoms competing with wisteria and magnolia
While wallflowers defy the odds through the cracks
As we wake to a haze of different hues
Clouds of natural confetti
Waft down in cascades of pink petals,
Fields of yellow and green and brown
Side by side
A coverlet of colour nestle
Beside hedgerows,
The days warm enough to venture out sleeveless,
The nights light for longer
Stepping out the door each moment into a living watercolour,
Of pink campion, bluebells, white cow parsley,
Skies of blue
Lawn daisies and buttercups,
Walks beside our seaside places
Torcross, Thurlestone, Mill Bay
What could be more glorious than a May day?
Throw the windows open
Sleep among the stars,
Birdsong will awaken us from our slumbers,
Black birds nesting and feeding,
My lovey-dovey and I would drive out on the moors
Stop for a cream tea
How could anyone want for anything more?

Oh please let me marry in May
Not yet of course
But one of these not too distant days!

Moon over Bowcombe

There's a little touch of magic in the sky tonight
Beautiful and tender
And only just partially eclipsed by the way I feel about you,
So I'm throwing the windows open wide
Along with my heart
On this night of nights
Where anything is possible
And I'm sending my wishes out into the vast star-lit heavens
And just hoping you're doing the same
And maybe some of those little wishes
Will turn into seeds
That will grow
And bloom
And turn this into something we can treasure
For tonight where everything is possible
everyone knows it takes two to make a wish come true
So I'll hold my hand to my lips
And blow this one to you!

For DJG

I dreamt of him last night
Strange because I wasn't even thinking of him,
But there he was
There we were,
A reunion of sorts,
He'd found me,
In some remote place,
My mentor,
The one who taught me about all things good,
He who handed me the keys
That unlocked the door
to greater discoveries
Fired a passion inside my brain
The passport to knowledge
The desire to want to learn
Again and again,
We were friends when I was very young,
Eleven I think, when it first started,
By the time I was thirteen
I was naturally passionately in love with him,
He bore it well
He told me firmly but kindly that any talk of that was out,
And we went on being friends till I was sixteen or thereabouts,
As if nothing had occurred,
I worshipped at his feet
Hung on his every word,
Seeped his intelligence in through my skin,
And loved him all the more
because I couldn't have him,

Can I help it if I have a romantic soul?
So we talked of literature instead,
And history
All things Greek,
He had travelled there many times,
And I shared his Hellenic passions,
I was with him in spirit on every journey he made,
I wonder what he'd make of me now,
He, in his dotage
And I, just starting to discover passions of my own,
And so the dream washed over me like soft Aegean waves
Like a Greek myth,
So much truth in the impossible,
Like two old souls destined to be together
Through this life and the next,
We sat in rapture
Talking of the old days,
And how as a child,
I had loved him,
Looked up to him with adoration
And drowned in those pale eyes,
Only to find myself pulled to the surface by his unseen hand,
In the dream we sat close together on the sofa
And he wrapped me in his ancient arms,
I loved him now as I loved him then,
With all the innocence of the child that used to stare at him from
the vast distance
Between his age and mine
But love isn't concerned with age,
Or the passing of the years,
Love isn't bothered about gender

Or looks,
To me he was perfect then as he is now,
To me he was my Mr Chips
My "To Sir With Love"
Mr Darcy, Mr Knightley
Heathcliff
All my literary heroes rolled into one,
Although he was never actually my teacher
He taught me so much
And I lived for those five O'clock tea-times
We had every afternoon with the rest of the neighbourhood,
Isn't it funny how a dream can make it all real again?
Explain what the logical brain cannot,
Resolve a lifetime of longing
In just one passing encounter
In the deep darkness of a summer's night.

On church steps

I left him at the church steps,
Little realising it would be the last time,
We would share our precious moments together
We made plans
to meet again
Later in the week,
And he left me longing for closer intimacies and adventures to
share
In his eyes I could see calmer harbours,
This beautiful chap of mine
How sweet was that week,
The beginning of something
I was certain,
Before fate intervened to draw the curtain
On the bright dawn of new beginnings,
The bloom nipped in the bud before it could blossom,
Falling on the pavement
Diminishing all hope
The rose striped of its petals
And alas he likes me not,
Perhaps he never did;
And now as I go up the street,
Hoping to catch a glimpse,
I am reminded of the places
Along the way where we used to meet
And the memories are bitter-sweet
You're spending your time on-line
But the messages you are sending are not mine,
As the ones I send you go unanswered,

What a delicate balance there is between being available and yet
unobtainable,
And all my good intentions
Cannot chase away
the shadows that surround you,
A sadness descends,
Knowing that you were the one
Who would have kept mine at bay,
Please open your heart,
Like you have the door,
So melancholy am
For the lack of your presence,
And my heart that I left at the church steps
When you walked away from me,
Taking away everything, I was dreaming of,
And it's going to take me some time
To get over the loss of you
And the loss of the dream
That was so very nearly mine.

I believe in romance

I believe in romance,
I believe in second chances
I believe that once every lifetime
Everyone dances to
That one special tune
With the one they truly love,
I believe in sunshine
I believe in silver linings
I believe there's a light shining
Even in the darkest of places,
I believe in leaving a candle
In the window
To guide the lost hearts home
I believe that we are never truly alone
I believe that one incredible day
That person will arrive
At my door
And I will want for no more
For that heart will marry mine
And we will be forever joined
Like two roses entwined
And we will spend the summer of our days together
And hold each other
When autumn comes
Wrapped in the depth and warmth of our affection
And when I look up, I will see you standing there
And we will smile because we will know we are each other's soul's
refection
My heart is impatient for your return

And how I yearn for just one moment in your company
To reassure me that it's all right,
I cling to this hope with all my might
I cannot face the reality that it may not
For while there's a chance
I will wait for that dance
For I believe in love
I have faith that one day you will cross the Rubicon for me,
One day you'll take that quantum leap
Until then I go to sleep
With your name on my lips before I turn out the light
And it's you I rush to meet in my dreams
For if I cannot be with you now
Then I hope someday.

4

Yesterday, Today and Tomorrow

Suspended in time

When I was a child
Time stood still
I could count the aeons
In the dust particles
That fell all about me and mixed with the chalk dust
And silence,
My favourite place was wandering around the deserted school
No teachers, no rules
I was like a little sprite
Inhabiting a secret place,
The school changed
As older I became
But still excuses I found
To hang around
Helping during the holidays
To retrieve books
from dusty
Stock rooms
For the term ahead,
And left alone with the dull light
I breathed in the books
And thought of the many generations of girls,
As I read names long forgotten written in the front cover
Who had thumbed through
The pages
Some with genuine interest
And others because they had to,
How many voices were heard
By these walls?

How many happy smiles
And the angst of the teenage years
Absorbed in these corridors?
How these feelings must be embedded in this space
And left in this place
When the girls left to join the human race,
And I became aware
That in the silence
a little part of those beautiful people
Were still here
All around me
And I was comforted,
In these walls they would be forever young.
I opened books at random pages
Read random paragraphs
Let the words fall gently around me
Sparking my imagination,
English literature
History
These were my opium,
I worshipped at the feet
Of my mentors
Those precious teachers
Who reshaped my world
Painted scenes so vivid
I could almost inhale the gun powder
Of the battle,
And during those unsure years
When everything was shifting around me
One thing was as clear as day to me,
I would lead the way,

And I knew from that moment
I would teach
I would write,
I would be an educator
A spark that set new minds alight,
And in the fullness of time
I took the path that was mine
And achieved that dream divine
My teaching days were my happiest
I knew I'd never find another calling like it.
I think of it often
And the person I once was,
I also remember my former self,
That child who found peace
In silent places
In the sanctity of words
In the stillness of just being,
When the minutes lasted a lifetime
Where time and dust mingled
And I, the silent witness
An interloper
In this blessed place.

On the death of Lenard Cohen

Blessed are the poets
Dylan and Cohen
Who speak to us in our darkest hours
For they have known
The depths of despair
They have known the imperfection of love
The inadequate, impotence
of the desperate heart
They have crawled to the altar
And sacrificed
Every precious essence of their souls
written their verses not in ink
but blood
So we can comprehend
The healing pain
Of the tortured,
Cry the tears of the deserted lover
In the agonising, dark and terrifying night
When loneliness holds your hand
And wolf strays too close to the door
Blessed are our heroes
For who will inspire us when they have gone?
Who will teach us to embrace
The longing,
The calling
The absolute agony of the spirit
When there is no relief, no release?
Who will push the boundaries
When our visionaries have entered

the bounds of immortality?
We will keep the music in our minds
As we weep into our hands
And look up into the firmament
In our sorrow
And thank them
For they have taught us to feel.
He is gone now, to find his Marianne.

The perfect happiness of a tomato sandwich

I always associate
tomato sandwiches with happiness.
Every lunch time
Of every day,
My grandad left his work in the industrial sites,
Stopping en route
To pick up half a loaf of freshly baked hot wholemeal bread
From Downings Bakery
Leaving his little car
In either Grey Street or Selborne Avenue,
And then pootling along to see Gran.
Together they would sit,
Tomato sandwich each
And a steaming hot cup of rooibos tea
taken from the shared pot
sitting snuggly between them
Dressed in Gran's knitted tea cosy.
The occasional spring onion
Or slice of cheese
Some fresh-picked lettuce perhaps,
Would sometimes fly into a sandwich,
But the basic recipe remained the same
Thin slices of garden grown tomatoes
From Grandad's plot,
Butter and a splosh
Of Worcester sauce,
Salt and pepper;
They would eat in companionable comfort

Jimmy and Anne,
My grandad and gran;
The food spread out
in front of them on Gran's rose painted china;
Starched white cloth,
Engaged in conversation;
And I, five or six years old at the time,
Would crawl under the little coffee table
And make myself very small,
Feeling like an intruder
On this very private daily ritual;
Playing with the door stopper doll,
Only coming out when Gran
Offered me a slice of homemade fruit cake.
Then with a peck of a kiss
planted on her lips,
And a pat on Rusty, the pointer's head,
Grandad would pop on his hat,
with a nod and a smile,
and head back to work.
They were married for sixty years
And I never once heard her complain
It was always the same
Tomato sandwiches and rooibos tea,
These always bring back happy memories for me,
Because it's the simple things, that make a marriage you see.

A mother's lament (and fathers too for that matter!)

I miss them when they never call
I miss them when they're far away
I miss them when I'm on my own
I miss them when I'm all alone
I miss them when I'm the last to know
I miss them when they always go
I miss them more than they'll ever guess
I miss them when they love me less
I miss them when they don't think of me at all
I miss them but still I walk tall
I miss them when I pretend I'm okay
I miss them when I have to face another day
I miss them even when they're thoughtless
I miss them when the situation is hopeless
I miss them when I see the others
I miss them when I wonder what I've done wrong
I miss them when I hear their song
I miss them every day
I miss them all month long
I miss them and it makes me sad
I miss them because I know
one day I won't be here
to miss them anymore.

The weather was warm

Gran's temper was hot
I was laying on the floor
Colouring my picture
Gran was busy,
didn't see and tripped over me
"Out!" Said she
"You're getting under my feet!"
I was heading for the door
Martha stopped me
"*Tackies* and sun hat, *picinini*!"
I was keen to be gone
moving restlessly from foot to foot
While she tied my laces
Planting the hat on my head.
Grandad was feeding the chickens and ducks
"Don't go near the mulberry trees, big snakes."
He called, going in with the eggs,
I made for the borehole pump
There was the tree there you see,
My safe haven for the day
I put a foot on its black trunk
And tried to heave myself up.
I pushed and pulled with all my might
My *tackie* got stuck
I tumbled in a heap
Lovemore was working nearby
He came running over from Gran's roses,
He reached down and picked me up
Dusted off the dry leaves

And placed me on the wooden plank
In the branches,
"Be careful, *picinini*, call me if you need to get down."
I looked around me
The dark green leaves wrapping me in cool shade
I could hear the old pump chugging away next door
As I reached for my first *naartjie*
peeled it with stubby fingers
Orange peels cascaded to the ground
Rusty was barking at me
"You can't come up here boy!"
I popped a segment in my mouth
Sweet juice hit my palate
I ate another and another
Loosing count, as the peels piled up
Orange pith under my nails
My belly was full
Lovemore came by and smiled
I threw him a *naartjie*
We ate together in complete silence
Then I said "Can you put me in the mulberry tree?"
He looked at me with concern,
"*Khulu* will be angry."
"But Lovemore!" I pleaded
"I will pick some for you."
He lifted me out of the tree.
We went over to the mulberry trees
Lovemore dropped the berries into my hands
We were eating and laughing
At our conspiracies
I was covered in purple stains

Martha was marching towards us
"Hey, wena!!"
She waggled a finger at Lovemore
As I was led away
Sent to my doom
Gran would be mad, Grandad would be sad
She dragged me into the house
"Into the bath!!"
"No, Martha!!"
I hated this more than a spank from Gran.
"Now, before they come back from the shops."
Martha scrubbed
"Ghou Madota! La gutshaya!"
Still moaning about Lovemore.
All evidence gone.
Fresh as a daisy
They found me colouring on the floor.
"Mulberries and cream for tea?"
"No thanks Gran, I have a sore tummy!"

Love from a distance

"I love you Mom, wish you were here."
Words I used to say on the phone,
I in England, my mother in South Africa.
Missed birthdays,
Mother's Day far away,
How her heart must have pined
I wonder how she felt when other mothers
Were taken out by their children
While she stayed at home alone again,
Two cards on the breakfast table
No one to give her hug
It was all given at a distance
The gifts we sent
Hardly a substitute for our presence,
The telephone calls a sad reminder
That we weren't there,
The family photographs
Memories when she was the cornerstone of our lives
The strong one
who nursed, drove, fed and patched,
I wonder who'll patched up her breaking heart
Now when her days are running out,
Absent children
Far off grandchildren she'll never know
not being able to share their lives,
or kiss them good night
Only at a distance,
And as the years roll by
Somehow, the holidays

we spend together are more about care-giving
The hours I spend drawing in the sun while she sleeps
Waiting for her to wake up,
preparing invalid meals I must fed her,
Soft white fish, mashed potatoes
A little of the old spirit still there
Doing the dutiful thing
Trying to cheer her up
Listening to her talk about old times,
Our days overshadowed by the knowledge
That I would soon be leaving
Travelling the eight thousand miles
Between her heart and mine
The desperate sadness at the airport
One last look
One last hug
One last touch
Tears on the plane
Not knowing when or if I'd see her again.
The phone call when I arrived.
"I'm home – safe and sound"
Mom's reply, "This is your home."
When we grow up and leave our mothers
We forget that just sometimes
They want to feel that we still need them
Like they need us.
They want to know that they are a special part of our lives.
And just sometimes we should let our mums be the child,
They've been the adults for so long
Brought us up
Seen us grow

And now we've let them go.
And so, not only on Mother's Day,
Remember to love your mom
Not just at a distance,
Call her while you've got the chance
Give her your time
Moms won't tell you how much they miss you
How they long to be a priority,
They hope you'll do that yourself,
And believe me when I tell you,
You should,
Because one day when yours has gone
Like mine,
You will hear yourself say
"I love you Mom, I wish you were here."
And you'll feel your heart break.

Conversations with the dead

When the ink has dried on the page
And they have led us to stories untold
Whispered tales in my ears
Whilst I slept,
Gentle nudges keeping me from harm,
And when, in dire distress
Answers came unexpectedly
To questions
that settled like a plague around my brain,
The comfort of a silent moment
Feeling someone near
And yet being completely alone,
All these things I have known.
When my tears gently fall
Like the waves lapping against the soft sands of memories,
I feel your heart beat in a song
You once loved,
And remember a happy time we shared
When we laid our weapons down
In our battle of wills
Just for the day.
Life carries us on
One moment at a time
We revel in its wonder
And shrink away in despair
We were so different you and I
And yet it's your emotions,
Your sentiment that carries me on
And when the chips are down

It's your name I call
I have always known my destiny
Was different to the one you imagined for me,
I am, you see, the writer
The chronicler
The teller of the tale,
In all its glorious ugliness
In all it's beautiful truth,
I am also an emotional wreck
The things I have experienced
A person should not have to deal with
Not as a young child
And not now
And so I ask for your leniency, Mother mine,
For stories cannot be sealed
And bottled to ferment
They will explode and break the vessel
That contains them.
I was put on this earth
Not to be a thorn
But a rose
I know you can see me
And I know through all your naked stubbornness
You understand
I think towards the end
We did reach some common ground,
Agreed to disagree
And while I can never accept your hard and cold outlook
I realise you were a product of your childhood
As I was a symptom of mine
I chose not to accept it

Like the 60s butterfly child that I was
I shunned your monotones
And reached for a more colourful palette
If that gave distress to you
I cannot apologise,
I was born into a larger family
I was always going to part of a bigger picture
And so I left you
To fulfil that destined role
I could not live in the shadow of fear
I had to move towards the light
And now I find myself dealing with all that's happened
I have come through to the other side
And dealt with the demons
And thanked my angels
So when you're all sitting up there
Pondering my life
Don't judge me too harshly
We all had our part to play.

On the passing of Hugh Masekela

Another of my heroes has gone to the far off Serengeti
in the skies
As I hear the haunting sounds of his golden horn
washing my ears in honey
The melodies from my childhood
Grazing in the Grass
The sounds of the cow bells
Takes me back to the grasslands of Matabeleland,
(Girl, you're a long way from home tonight)
Far from cattle and the kraals
And the sunsets in the Matopos
And sitting beside the dam on a hot afternoon
Village children running to open the gate
Where they came from
Who could tell?
Arriving right on cue when you needed them.
Driving home, the wind blowing through my hair
A cold beer in the jazz club
In Cement House
Pleasant mornings listening to my favourite radio presenter
Playing Happy Hanna
Toe-tapping my way through the day
A spring in my step
Such a happy interlude in my life
When everything was possible
And love was a blissful dream away
My happy go-to tune
It takes me straight back there.
African Breeze

Reminds me of hitting the clubs in the capital
Cruising down Lomagundi Road
On a warm summer's evening
The music washing over me
My dapper lover by my side
just knowing the night was going to be amazing,
Hugh at the Gracelands Concert
Paul Simon introducing him
Bring Back Nelson Mandela
The crowd swaying and taking in the man, the legend, the
ambassador, activist
Still an exile in his country then
Zimbabwe, the closest he could get to home
I, a face in the crowd
The best concert I've seen
How calm and happy everyone was
The atmosphere one of peace
And brotherhood,
Reminding us that love conquers all.
I went alone and joined with my country men and women
Just lapping up the music
The performance of Coal Train – Stimela
Where we held a collective breath
A sad chapter in history
And with his one-time love,
Miriam Makeba
Soweto Blues
Taking to the stage
A musical collaboration so powerful
So united,
Music has no borders.

No More Crying,
A song by Hugh to his lover
As he leaves her to go on the road.
And Lizzy
Where he begs to go with his girl
S'thandwa Sami
We cannot go with him
But tonight he leaves behind thousands of breaking hearts
For this true son of Africa,
Who brought joy and hope into the lives
Of his fellow countrymen and women,
could paint a picture with his music
And conjure up imagery so powerful
You can remember what it was like to be there at that special
moment.
Fare thee well, Hugh
Hope we meet you when we get there
Till then we'll always have Kalahari Nights in the *shebeen*.

For my son

I always dreamed I'd have a son
Someone to carry on the name
Someone to love,
Someone to ease the pain,
You arrived with the dawn,
As the sun slipped into the sky
On a lucky Friday in June
My Gemini twin,
An early birthday present,
A sweet, special tune,
On your own wonderful day,
And so you started early
Doing things your way,
And from the moment you came along
My life has been a happy song,
You brought blessings and sunshine,
Beloved child of mine,
What angel divine
Brought our two lives together
Mine and thine?
Now you are all grown
With a sweet boy of your own,
But well I remember those beginning days,
Away in your dreams,
Your milky breath
As you slumbered near
So close that I could hear
Your heartbeat,
While I cradled your head on my arm,

So contented was I to watch over you
Keeping you from harm.
Then as you grew older
And inhabited your own
Space
Still I checked on you as you slept
And whispered a prayer
Of protecting grace.
For my blessed boy,
Whose beautiful smile
Was all I wanted when home I came,
And so I tried to make the world a better place,
To bring happiness to that adorable, little face
And when our story began
It was just you and I
Although time brought many different characters into play,
But through it all
You brought a calm, peaceful, reassuring presence
In a story of turmoil and despair
You were always there,
And for this I thank you, dearly loved son,
For without your love and support
I doubt I'd have made it.
The one true and constant thing
Who made life worth living,
A warm embrace from you was all that was needed
To clear the clouds and to make the sun come out again,
And if there is only one thing
A parent could ever ask for,
It is that at least one child of theirs
Is a true reflection

Of their life's endeavours.
To be able to say
"I did one thing right."
For you, dear son, can never know how lonely I was
And how you filled that gaping, empty space
With warmth, love and joy.
And so light of my life,
Sunshine of my soul,
The person who took all my fragmented pieces,
Scooped them up
And made them whole,
I wish you health and happiness
Always,
And especially on this day
This blessed, blessed day
When in one rapturous moment
You came my way.
And so changed my name from other
To Mother
And the world would never be the same
For from that time on,
We had a Timothy
And all was well with me.

Two sisters

I knew two sisters many years ago
When I was but a tiny girl
In Convent Blues.
The older one, was the same age as I
Confidence shone out from every pore of her olive-kissed skin,
Where I was shy,
They came from a far off exotic place
Not of my race,
They were noble,
The royal bloodline of kings,
And I found myself under a spell
Halva,
Tins of olive oil
How far they had travelled
Who could tell,
In the days when foods
Like these were not common fare
They had them there
In their home
Where I frequently ate
Unexpectedly appearing at their gate
Mama looked after the children
And Daddy sold cars,
We played together,
Counted the stars,
Patched up our grazes and scars
I swopping one sister for the other
Depending on who I found,
The older sister was studious and sound

The younger more carefree;
Innocent happy pursuits entertained us,
The day we went to see the horses
Daddy paid for lessons,
I tagged along,
Sticky from molasses
Someone suggested we upturn the empty water tank
So there we were
the three of us
Running for all we were worth
While the corrugated tank
Rolled down the hill
Shrieking and green from
Being turned around and around.
How I loved those friends
But separate ways
We went at thirteen
To different high schools
And divided we were
After a seven year stretch
I thought my heart would break,
The younger sister and I were to cross paths in later years
And with the meeting
Brought fresh tears
As she dated the only boy I loved
It wasn't her fault
But it hurt that she was his choice,
My foolish pride and my mother's harsh rules
Stood in the way of young love
But I blamed her nonetheless
For her thoughtlessness
When everyone knew Charlie was mine.

On Women's Day
(For all my sisters)

Before you ask me out
Remember I am someone's mother
Someone who respects me
Who loves me
Who has placed me above,
I have been through the joy
Of conception, procreation
And giving life to a child
I have lived for the love of my children
And felt the panic
Late in the night
Wondering if they were all right,
I have held them when they were sick,
And laughed with them when they were well,
I have been a lover, a wife,
A sister and a daughter
Trusted you with my life
Given you my heart,
Before you see me as a sexual object
Remember I am someone's grandmother
A little someone
Who looks up to me
To set the example
I won't give you my body
Until I give you my love
And I expect the same from you
I won't give you my heart
Until I know you are for real,

You'll have my brothers to deal with.
I believe in commitment
I believe in a love that lasts
I have loved and lost
I have held a hand in the dark
Confessed my secrets,
I believe in upholding all my sisters
Even those not of my genetic makeup
For we all have different stories to tell
We all have different threads to add to this tapestry
Called life,
I am menopausal
I cry a lot
I love deeply and hold on to the smallest slight,
I don't forgive lightly
Hurt me and you hurt my soul
My values are what make me
Who I am.
If you can meet me on these terms
I will put my trust in you
I am proud of who I am
I own the path I have walked.
I am woman
And if you're going my way
I will take your hand.

The good ole boys of Klipdrift

On wagons they came across the veld
To the outer reaches of the North West Cape,
Hostile tribesmen awaited,
And through rough terrain
Did they cut their course.
In oil skins up to their knees in water
Did they dig and scrape
Through the Vaal's sticky mud
Though the water be cold
Their endeavours to find and hold
That elusive little gem
Drive them on
And means survival for another few months
Where mouths can be fed
Out there in the wild.
And bent they were with their sifting pans
The alluvial muck to dig
And shovel,
For a shining stone
Or a little pebble,
A crown for a king
Or a pile full of rubble.
And markets rose and fell
But through the sweltering hell
our ancestors toiled
And laboured
To discover the stones hidden in the soil,
For jewellery shops far from home.
And they were not rich

And they were not wealthy
But they were ruddy
And rough and healthy
And gold they had not any
Just determination
And grit aplenty.
And they came from the Emerald Isle
And places across the sea
These young men of ours
And married the Dutch *meisies* and brought forth
Their own sons and daughters.
And so, families began, and continued to be
As generations of progeny
Worked with the stones
And they lived in corrugated shacks.
Coldest winters
And blazing hot sun.
And we are fascinated by their stories
And their former glories
And we want to study and learn
Where our roots come from.
And so we salute them and thank them for everything
That we are.
They were true pioneers in every sense of the word
Trail blazers
Who made a life in a virgin land,
And they danced Irish jigs
And wove wonderful tales,
How many were truth
And how many were fiction
Who could tell?

And little do we care
As we listen with wide-eyed wonder.
And to my family
And my blessed genealogy
I am proud
For they are the true precious diamonds in this tale
That I have found.

I know I don't say it enough

Because it embarrasses you
Now that you're all grown up
But I love you, son.
You are the one thing in my life
That demonstrates how wonderful the love of the Lord has
been to me,
And I know you are not religious
And I know you think I'm a soppy, menopausal mummy
But to love a child and get that love back
Is worth so much more
Than all the gold in the world
And all the diamonds in the earth's crust
The miracle of birth
Watching your baby grow into a little person
An individual in his own right
But with a reflection of his father and his mother in his eyes,
In his smile,
A child created
When love was at its beautiful height,
And when I look at you and your boy
Please know you are my heart's delight,
And that special song I always play,
for you truly are
The Sunshine of My Life,
I know you are busy
As am I,
But there is a time in every day
When I think of you
And give thanks to Heavenly Father

For giving you to me.
And my happiest days
And the sunniest moments in my life
Have been spent in your company.
None of us know what life
Will bring
And so we make the best of each day
And we thank the universe
For everything we are given
A seed is planted
And it grows
We have no idea what will blossom
And what will not
But I can honestly say
The day you came into the world
the heavens were smiling down on me,
And so my life was blessed
Then, now, forever,
For no matter where I go
I will always know
That you will be there.
And one day when I am no longer here
You will feel my presence
And read my words
And know that it is just part of a bigger plan
And realise that you are truly loved
And always will be.
Life is brief
So much to achieve
With the limited time allotted
I am a mere apprentice

Striving for a purer spirit,
Thank you for teaching me
How to be a parent
And that to love a child is the greatest gift I could have ever been given.

These four little buttons
(For our Michael)

These four buttons
I found in my drawer
bought a long time ago
kept for something special
For someone special
And now the time has come.
They will do very nicely
For the soft jumper
Just finished knitting
To keep a little darling warm
Buttoned up against the cold.
I watch him as he sleeps
All wrapped up in blue
And I remember his daddy
Many years ago
In a similar pose
When I checked his breathing
Every five minutes or so
Something I never stopped doing
Even when he was a much older lad.
Now I do the same
With this little one.
Mum and Dad are out shopping
And I have been left in charge
What a precious sight he is,
Away in his dreams!
And I too, am at peace with the world
With this little chap

Created in love
Waited for, wished for
And prayed for.
I wonder what goes on in his mind
Active little sleeper!
Suckling movements
And little eyes blinking
Even his hands are not still
Clutched around my finger
What a joy it is to watch him
I have no greater pleasure
No desire to be anywhere other than here,
The house is still as I too am still,
Content, happiness abounds
In the soft light
As I listen to his breathing
The rise and fall of his chest
I whisper a little prayer of thanks.
Promise to be his guardian
And hope that I am granted enough time on this earth to see
him grow into a man.
I look forward to the day when he will escort me to town
Look after me, a frail old dear
And say no one messes with you, *Gogo*,
I am here to see you safely home.
Oh how blessed am I
To share this time with this little guy
How cherished is he, to me
And how lucky to have found a use for those four little buttons
For they bind us closely together,
His mum, his dad, Michael and me.

The child on the veranda

I came upon a little girl
I guessed her age to be about four or so
She'd climbed up the wall on the veranda
And was watching the world go by
Waiting for something
Waiting for someone,
She beamed when she saw me
Although she didn't know me
Something inside us both drew us together
An inner force neither of us understood
I felt the longing in her,
And saw it in her beautiful, clear, clean blue eyes
The kind that reflect the light
Her little turned up nose
The tip sunburnt and slightly peeling
As she sat there on the edge of the wall
Surrounded by sunshine,
I noticed her yellow cotton handmade dress, ribbons in her hair,
It made me realise someone loved her
but yet here she was alone
Braided hair, just beginning to grow.
As I came up to her she reached out her arms
And I went to her.
We embraced.
"It's going to be all right," I told her,
"I love you and together we will survive."
And as she nuzzled into my neck
Tears moist against my skin,
I felt the most overwhelming feeling of love

Emanating from her to me
And I reflected it back to her.
I saw through her pain
Raw, incomprehensible
The arguments she'd witnessed
Mommy crying, Daddy walking out.
The banjo he used to play,
Her mother's mandolin
So melodic and melancholy,
The wooden coat hanger that broke in her tiny hands,
the anger she experienced.
The song on the radio.
I know how she felt when her father left
I saw her mother's tears
I know long she waited on that veranda
Looking out,
Waiting for him to come back
Because I was there.
I felt the rejection, the abandonment,
And I understood the longing in those eyes
The deep need to be loved
That she carried like a suitcase strapped to her back,
The pain of separation,
The loss of her parent.
It is only when the future meets the past
that healing in the present can begin,
I loved that little child
I know her secret anguish
And how she hid it behind a perfect smile
And how through it all
I knew she'd persevere,

Now the years have passed
And when she looks in the mirror
She no longer pretends it didn't happen,
I'm proud of this life I have lived
And that the one person that child relied on
never let her down
That child, you see
was me.

There is no concept of time in the land of darkness

Night is endless
It stretches on and on
Like the blinding pain
And waves of nausea that wrack my brain
As I drift in and out of sleep
Reaching for a splash of water to moisten my tongue
From the dryness that never ceases
Until the nausea hits once more
And I lose it again.
The hammer strikes the anvil
The vice tightens around my temples
As I apply pressure to numb the effect
Pushing, pulsating, thumping
I feel like banging my head against the wall
Somewhere between madness and desperation.
Drugs useless
They offer false hope.
The cat checks on me periodically
Gently lifting a paw to my lips to check I'm still breathing
I wish I could train her to massage my forehead
When she's really worried she snuggles into my neck
Or lays on my chest
Feeling it rise and fall
It reassures her that I'm still alive,
And when I have the strength,
I crawl to kitchen to give her food
Let her out and hope she returns before I collapse once again.
Bless her, she only has nine lives

I, it would appear, have more
For I have a thousand times knocked at death's door
And just when I think I can take no more
I am turned away and live to see the light of another day.
Weakened by the starvation of 36 hours
This episode has been the worst
I clear away a mountain of tissues
The bucket of puke
Change the sheets;
Dry as a parched desert
I swallow and clear my throat
I try a little sustenance,
Pull the curtain a little aside
The brightness flashes before me
Eyes sensitive
Head tender
The throbbing not quite at an end,
But starting to subside,
Perhaps I'll stay indoors today
Semi dark, semi light
Slow and slower.
How many days of my life have I lost to this debilitation,
And how more to come?
I can't take much more of this pain
How much longer before I go insane?

In loving memory of my mother

When feathers float down from heaven
I know that you are nearby
I hear your name in the breeze
And in the leaves that flutter about me
In the eaves where the birds gather
And in the corner of the garden where
the crocuses push out of the ground in the spring
I am aware of the subtleties of the new seasons
Which have been sent to give me fortitude.
And especially on the days when I am facing another battle
That is when I feel your presence and it gives me strength to continue
And although I can no longer feel the comfort of a hug
you visit me often;
I think you would be proud of how I'm coping.
Catching a glimpse of something seen but not quite seen,
I imagine you,
Standing there in the doorway observing my life's little scenes
The falling dusk casting shadows
That's when I smile and acknowledge you.
And when I find myself with a difficult choice or need to be
reminded of my worth
You send me a sign
A rainbow, a shove out of harm's way
A friend's kindness to help me through the day.
I have learnt to listen now
And just to observe
And take notice of those strong feelings
Because I realise it's you guarding me, guiding me and helping me
from a place beyond mine.

You are just out of my vision of sight
But I know you are there
watching over me as I sleep
Coming to me in dreams
And on the days when illness sits upon me
I cry out to you
(for you were my comforter, nurse and nurturer)
You are there to help me through the malaise.
I have lived my life because of you
And so, as another anniversary rolls around
I will celebrate your life by adding light to the cathedral's dark spaces
Bringing blossoms to the churchyard
And let your candle give hope and peace
to all weary travellers who pass this way
For the love of your spirit has saved me from all the harms
of this world.
And now when I see a shadow pass over me
Or shiver for no reason
I need not fear
For I have your protection
You are ever near.
Loving, kind angel
You are not far
And will never be forgotten.
And when I too stand on that bridge
That connects this world with the next
You will be there to walk across with me.
And so precious one
I leave these flowers in your memory
And shed a little tear
For you are gone another year.

As we pass the 18th door

As we pass the 18th door
The day you were born
I thought we had time,
I never thought at sixteen, I would see you no more,
When I first held you in my arms
I promised to protect you from harm
And saw your helplessness and knew that I had to be upright and strong
To teach you right from wrong
But weeks and months and years passed us by
And as you grew you looked to me
As parent, teacher and friend
And not once did I falter
For a mother's love never alters
It is a perfect state of purity
Unquestionable, unconditional, absolute
When night after night I spent in a delirium of broken sleep
Because you wouldn't settle
And the teeth would not come
The jobs I lost, mattered not to me
when the fever was wracking your tiny body
And the only thing that would sooth you
Was the milk from my breast
Because you were more important than the wrath of an employer
Who would never know that feeling
Of a child's utter dependency
And the responsibility
So overwhelming that swallows
A person whole;
The primeval desire to nurture and keep you from hurt

Overtakes a parent's very being.
But you were different
That I could see
And had a will of your own.
From an early age you wanted to do things in your own way.
a loving and sweet-natured child
Nonetheless
And in my heart I knew you were special
Spending pocket money on crystals
Not sweets like your friends.
Reading your books
Living in your world of fantasy
Because the real one was too daunting.
Then there was that terrible fateful day
you slipped from my grasp
And turned your heart away
A mother no longer needed
Made redundant from a position
I thought would be mine forever
Impenetrable, was the wall you built around you
And I cannot not breakthrough the lines that you have drawn,
The terms you have made are impossible
So I walked away
For what else can a tender heart do?
And so it is thus,
I live my life and you live yours
Our paths have not crossed although we probably step over each
other's footprints every day in this small town
And as you start this adventure called life
With ideals of your own,
I wish you well

I will continue the payments for a person I no longer know until
you come of age.
And although I think of you often
(As often as the minutes in the day)
As that sweet child that was once so much a part of my life
although is now so altered I would probably not recognise,
I hope that this bitterness in you will pass
For if it does not it will eat away at you.
And one day if you ever think of me without prejudice
And find peace
Then I hope you will remember the mother who tried to give you
everything,
Who only saw the best in you
Even when you could not
I hope you will think hard on it,
For while you were so busy thinking of reasons not to love
I was trying to keep the pieces of my heart from falling and
shattering to the ground.
And as for time, it passes so quickly
Choices come with consequences
And when my allotted years are all spent
I hope you won't regret
That hot-headedness of youth
When you believed you were right
For when you have lived a little in this world
You will find that things are rarely black and white
But fall into many shades of uncertainty
Experience teaches us best
And remember that I make up half of your DNA
You can deny it if you like
But it's there

And if you are the person I believe you to be
You will one day face what you have done,
On your own, without the sentiments of others
And realise that the weight of your decision was not worth
the cost
For the mother you lost.
Perhaps then you will be ready to find me.
Until then I must live the life
others have tried to destroy
And my reputation that I have worked so hard to establish,
While I pick myself up each day and try to make the best of it.
It's tragic that it came to this.
Those fears you have whether you feel they are real or imagined
have no substance,
And in time you will realise this
I think in your heart of hearts you already know this
So on your 18th birthday
I will grieve your loss once again
And respect your wishes and keep away.
I hope you're spending it well
And as I look back on your entry into the world many years ago
And the silent tears I have cried
I will remember that little girl I was heaven blessed to once
call my own.

My mother's eyes

From the moment I first remembered
I recall those beautiful eyes of green
And the light that danced behind them.
Many sorrowful rivers washed over those precious stones
For she was sentimental to the bone,
Took every slight as a deep mortal wound
This Mother mine.
Often in quiet times I would find her
In strange reflection,
Tears streaming down from hidden depths
Far beyond my childlike comprehension
And I would wonder what had made her so sad.
Those eyes saw everything but kept them locked in.
Hiding secrets, we would never see,
Passion, jealousy and pain
Laughter, sunshine and rain
Somehow, she knew what I was about,
No use trying to deny it
Or being creative with the truth
She saw through my thin veil of deception.
So, I put any untruth
under a self-protecting cloak where it remained and grew until it
could hide no more.
The things she nursed over the years
The betrayal of her true love
Her daughter's rebellion,
A soldier son,
Under a virescent mantle.
Spent her years in melancholy mood

And only sometimes would the green pixies escape and play under the moon
And then would she twinkle and sparkle
And show some of her inner authentic self,
Magical and mysterious
In a far-off place;
Playing a soul-stirring melody on her beloved mandolin
I loved her best
Tossing away her worries with a carefree abandon
Talking fondly of days gone by
Younger youthful days on a grandmother's farm
The love of cousins
Love's first fever;
Then she would pull me close to her heart and we would fall asleep in the afternoon sun.
I was more grateful for those times than any others
It was much more pleasant than to stand in judgement
Waiting for the verdict on my actions
This is when I felt truly loved.
For while she dreamt, she was at peace.
Her eyes closed to the suspicions that plagued her waking hours.
I loved my mother's eyes
The soft green waves that pulled me in and pushed me away,
That made me feel happy, that made me feel alone
The lighthouse beam
That led me home.

The little things we collect

Never in my life did I expect to feel like this
So utterly bereft
like a bone chewed and spat out
No sweet meat left,
Dry like sinew
Emotionally drained,
grief that is absolute
As the end chugs along to its unhappy conclusion,
I am faced with someone else to grieve for.
Never to be seen again
That person I lay with, fought with, once loved
Is no more
I have nowhere to direct my hate, channel my frustration
He lives but in a different form.
We spent half a lifetime living in a combat zone
Enemies till the last.
Now we stand court-martialled
and the jury is still out on this one.
Doors closed on rooms no longer used
Sashes drawn on windows where no one will look in
Stuff put in boxes and shoved in a loft
All our memories
Collecting spider's cobwebs and dust in the darkness
We were a moment in time
Suspended along with the unwanted detritus of our lives
Remnants of what used to be.
As we move into the space of a single bed, single bank accounts,
TV suppers for one,
In our lonely desperation.

I left, that much is true,
Walked out when I realised we both deserved more
We had made each other miserable for too long
Drowning in regret, recriminations
Festering resentment
It was the right thing to do.
Now in the cold light of a sunless morning
I face it full on,
We collect many things in life
Photographs, momentums of precious moments
Cluttered ornaments on our shelves .
Cheaply made curios from holidays,
Things we convince ourselves mean something.
But when that vase falls and breaks into fragments
We rush to catch it yet it shatters nonetheless
And when we pack away our lives
These things are thrown away by our children
Who despise us for our sentimentality.
"Do you want Mom's sun flower vase?"
"No, I never liked the hideous thing."
Why do we cherish them so?
Surely it's the emotions we should treasure?
How someone came along with a hug at that precise moment
when our world was falling apart;
A friend walking through the door bringing sunshine and
warmth when the day had turned grey,
But what about the despair we carry?
The sorrow and the hurt
How do we deal with that?
Where do we leave behind, that excess baggage?
The death of a relationship is so final.

Once you walked into my world and saved me completely,
Wrapped me in your arms and loved me with wild and crazy abandon;
Jealous with passion
Drunk on love,
Now we take our amphetamines elsewhere.
He is gone, that man
She is gone too to another life in another world.
I once had a husband
And he had a wife.
Nobody would believe that now.
I never wanted to get married
I fought for years to avoid it
A standing joke in the family
My brother told everyone I was afraid of nothing except marriage.
Not because I didn't want to say "I do"
But because I didn't want to face the inevitable "this"
Divorced from someone, something I once held dearest to my heart
Why did it come to this?
Where was that bend in the road, the point of no return?
And what makes us doomed to fail?
Who can possibly tell?
Yesterday is in the past.
And the shared experiences have been filed away under "Obsolete."

The departing of a friend

Close the door,
And quietly take your leave,
I don't want to watch as you go,
I can't look at your face
With distance in your eyes
As you stride forth to pastures anew,
Leaving behind this bundle,
I will now carry on my back
The colour of deepest blue.
How misery sits upon me in abundance,
How I'll grieve for the ghost of you
When your aura is all that's left in the room
after you're gone.
Will I still see it in the gloom?
The imprint you've left on the cushions,
The stain of your coffee cup on the table
How long will they remain when you are not able?
When I close my eyes will I pretend I can still hear your music
playing on in my memory
when your image is everything I cannot see?
What comfort will it bring?
Will I reminisce about a time when your songs began my every
working day?
And the only reward I wanted to continue the endless toil of a
long and dull afternoon.
They not much consolation now in the emptiness of this space.
My voice cannot reach you and you will not answer.
The spoken word is hardly a substitute for a lost caress.
Desperation I will not demonstrate,

Neither tears will you see
Although there will be plenty.
These will be mine and mine alone to keep,
When your desertion starts to seep.
Capture my smile now
And remember me as I wish you well.
Think not for one minute how I will cope
Without you, without hope.
For it matters not that you go,
But that you came.
So, I shall not drown
Nor take to drink
When left alone to think,
But rejoice in time.
Take my devotion with you,
I have no use for it,
It belongs not to me
And farewell, dear love,
With all my gratitude
My fondest affection follows and provides fortitude for the
journey unseen.
Remember me sometimes and where we've been.
Don't wander too far
For one day our paths are sure to meet.

For the love of a lad

Last night I dreamt I was walking with a little boy
He held me by the hand and led me through the lane
And the cat followed close behind
Chattering as we went
Greeting neighbours over fences.
He was a clever boy, this young one with wide eyes
As we spoke of intricate and complicated things
And yet they seemed so logical to this enquiring mind
and we were much at ease, this little fellow and I,
And I felt content
And life was complete,
A circle interwoven between my life and his,
We were connected in more ways than just our biological tie.
And that soft realisation that love comes in many shapes and sizes
And sometimes it's not what you imagine it to be,
But what it was meant to be,
The best possible option.
This child of my dreams will arrive,
For the future has been foretold
And I have been shown
For now, he is in his spiritual home,
And my ancestors know him and call him by name.
I must wait for him,
Son of my son.
This beautiful young love.
How long did we wait for you?
A grandmother's prayers,
Daily sent up to the Father above
For care, health and love.

So, when you arrive, I will know you are the special one
The promised one,
Holding you close to my heart
And cherishing this cherub
Ours
For always
A little soul companion
summer sunshine and autumn rain
Our adventures will be things of fun
And memories we'll make
This little guy and I
As we traverse our little world
For now, Patience is called for
To let time do its bidding
For I cannot rush his coming
For while he sleeps, he grows
And when the time is right
He will emerge into this world
And life will begin.
For him it will all be new
And for me in the burnished sunset years
It will be a second chance
To love, to learn, to wonder.

The keeper of memories

Life has lead me down some strange paths,
People have come and touched my heart,
Made times better and sometimes worse
But still friends have come
to open the door
And coax me out
Even on the days when I would rather retreat
I have learnt not to say no
Not to any invitation
For they have taken the time
To think of me
When they could have asked someone else,
And always I am enriched by the outing
Fed from the inside out,
And their intentions may not be clear at the time
And sometimes I feel they are doing it for just for me,
But I have learned that this may not always be the case,
Maybe they need me
As much as I need them?
And so when someone reaches out
And says let's go here
Or can we go there
Say yes!
Leave the inertia behind,
Even though it may be the last thing you want to do,
Put your warm things on,
Brave the elements
And close the door to your warm hearth
It will be there waiting on your return,

So just for the night,
Just for a few hours
Go together
Enjoy the company
Bathe in the glow
For just some day
You just don't know,
That friend who knocks on your door
May no longer be there,
And you will be the poorer for it.
So while you have the chance
Live your moments
Share the warmth and experiences
For it is you they seek
You they want
Because you are their memory-keeper
And you will remember
Even when they cannot.

For Tilly

I loved her from the start
With all my heart,
We met quite by chance
At the college
Where I wanted classroom experience.
That receptionist will never know
What happened next and how her simple instruction
"Go upstairs there's a class up there,"
Would change the course of my life forever,
I knocked
And a door opened
A door to another portal
A different world,
And there she was
Untidy hair,
Craft materials strewn here and there
In chaotic display
"I've come to help"
"Good, we need you!"
And so it started
The gentle teaching she taught me,
Patience and love
For our beautiful pupils
Whose various abilities
Set the pace,
And bit by bit my horizons
Expanded
The books we talked about
The places we went

Concerts and readings
Songs that will live with me always,
The memories she evoked,
The moments we shared
Through darkness and light
My agony aunt,
and friend,
To the end,
Who showed me that the joy of life
Is to treat each day like it's your last;
And so we always have the cake
And lemon sorbet
Because we know time is short
And it's all we've got,
These tiny, precious grains
Falling, falling into the bottom half of the hourglass,
None of us know
How long it will last
And the love of a true friend
is ever enduring,
There are times when we may not agree
Times when we feel we've let each other down
But an argument is nothing
And matters not one jot
In the grand scheme
When two like-souls share a connection
A link that transcends this life
And into the next,
For what are we
When it's all said and done
But pure essence

And when someone looks into your soul and says I know you
And you know me
And we are friends
Because we chose to be,
That's all that matters.
We are all falling particles
of sand and dust,
Falling, falling, forever falling,
But it's only when the light catches the dust
That we find illumination, true enlightenment.

Green eyes
(For my niece, Michelle)

Green eyes tell of little sighs
Pain and lies
That brought tears to those little eyes
And an aunt who wasn't there
Who went AWOL
And who fought hard to win
Her love,
Her trust,
As we must for our own;
Our flesh, our blood,
Our kith and kin,
Last seen a babe in arms
And the gulf of years between us
And the guilt that came
Not protecting her from
Hurt and harm,
In the troubled years
When she would have benefited from that love,
A little balance
A different side to the tale,
How can we ever bridge the gap
Of all that we've lost?
So we move forward
And an opportunity found us
Together in London Town,
And so to meet,
Our first breakfast,
Trying hard to find our feet,

And over coffee and eggs,
I looked into those pools
Of fire and stone
And realised they were of our own,
For her eyes were so like those of another
Those of my own dear mother,
Who would have from heaven's doors
Been smiling on this happy scene,
At her daughter captivated by those beautiful eyes of green,
For this much missed granddaughter
Now found,
Restored to the bosom of my love,
And her eyes quite serene
When all the awkwardness was gone.
And so the circle is continued
And hearts once torn apart
Can now start
To heal
As we reach across the void
And fill that empty space with love,
Acceptance
And a knowledge
That this is where we belong,
Together, reunited,
The wrongs of the past righted,
Between the two of us,
For it was not our war,
And another pair of eyes
Filled with tears of joy,
And as the time draws close
And I remember the anniversary of my mother's passing,

I am thankful I can still see a reflection
In those blessed jewels passed down
From one generation to the next
And know that we are heaven blessed,
And those who left this life with so
Much torment
Can now be left to rest
For we found peace,
And I say a silent prayer
And thank the universe for the gift of a niece.

Soft-spoken words

As I sit beside the ocean
In this land faraway
I think of those in my life
As a silent prayer falls off my lips
"Thank you."
For all the secrets I've kept
Safely locked away in my heart
"I love you."
For the chance to make a difference again tomorrow
To say the words we say almost in a whisper
To those who must hear
To make the message clear,
"I miss you."
These are the feelings that are unique to me
And the boundless love that dwells in this woman's walls,
And as I watch the waves ripple on the shore
I couldn't love you more
My first born son,
My only grandson,
A much beloved daughter in law,
My brothers, a sister
And friends of my bosom
Sisters of my soul
My kith, my kin
Cousins of my bloodline
Near and far,
Lovers, real and imagined,
I have had it all,
And for the kindness of random strangers.

And if for some reason
I don't make it back
To England's fair isle
Know this
You were well loved by me,
When I cease to breathe your air,
When I am no longer there,
When my life is done,
Please remember you made me joyful,
Gave me the happiness I could never have hoped to possess,
And if I kept these things to myself
It is because they are precious gems to me,
Let this verse be my epitaph
I came to love
And so I leave my energy behind,
I hope the universe will make good use of it,
And as I leave one final word,
And send it out on the breeze,
"I am always with you."
When you think of me,
Miss my smile,
The eyes that wept silent tears
Over the love of you,
Please read my words,
Say them out loud,
This is my legacy,
My poetry my book of love,
my gift to you.

The old love letter

I found an old love letter,
How you promised to be true
How no one else would do,
The rapture in your eyes
Whenever you looked at me and how I was all you would see,
All you would want,
How quickly we forget,
How soon those promises turn to lies,
And whenever I heard you speak
Those breathless sighs
Turned into alibis,
And the life I tried to make for us
Were just dreams built on sand
The thread of gold that bound us together,
Till my hands were left bleeding and bruised from all the years of
trying to patch and mend
the holes in the fabric,
So I could no longer hold the needle,
No longer see to thread it,
For all the tears in my eyes,
You took what you wanted
Stole from me
half of my heart
Took my voice,
Until all I had was my integrity
My dignity
And the will to pick myself up and walk away,
I hold the love letter in my hand
And commit it to the fire

It is consumed by the flames
It crumples and turns to ash
And so I am purged by the embers
I walk away free,
But will you ever be free from what you did to me?

The silk scarf

The silk scarf you once wore
Now lies upon the floor
It carries your fragrance like an enchanting spell
Even though you no longer are here to dwell,
And the roses that bloomed in June
When we walked in the haze of that afternoon
Are merely petals strewn
Where your feet once walked
And the hours we talked,
But you wanted none of it,
None of me
And passions denied
Unlike the blooms that fade
When summer wanes,
Only gain momentum
And burn more fiercely,
Just like the ghost of your presence that lingers on and on
And mocks me when you've gone
And the memory of the thrill,
Will last until
I can no longer remember
All the songs you played,
How we would have loved
If only you had stayed,
The seduction of the violin's sad lilt
And the cello's notes
Like the ripples on a pond,
Of you, I am so fond,
All the poems I wrote

That you will never read,
While my heart quietly bleeds;
The sentiments were true
They were meant only for you,
And I could never understand why
In the blink of an eye
You turned your mind away,
What was it that you found so unappealing?
Was my depth of feeling
too much for you to take
And my genuine emotion
All a mistake?
Your silence speaks volumes
And although I long for you
I know it cannot be,
For it won't ever be me,
For whom your heart beats,
And so our palms will not meet
And we will not walk
Side by side like we did that day,
For you have chosen to go your own way,
So the scarf will lie where it will
And I will go on loving you still.

From now until then

Promise you'll look for me in eternity
For I will love you till then,
And deny it if you must,
But you have loved me too,
There was no earthly reason
Why we came to be;
In a different time and place
Our love would have been outlawed
And somehow
In that moment in history
It happened,
Defying all logic,
We knew we should be
And what we created lived on
For all to see
For he is more beautiful than you or me
And his progeny a prefect reflection of everything innocent and good,
And so we must accept our coming together as something
predestined,
For the maker of these things is all knowing,
And the soul is wiser than the mind,
And those who dare, stronger than the timid;
Although we never formally exchanged vows,
Marriage unnecessary
In a love such as ours,
For we always were
As we will always be,
We recognise mates of our souls the moment we met them,
For our fate has been decided many aeons ago.

Beginning

I was shown a place,
Where many people were gathered
And I recognised each and every one,
Everybody, every face,
Smiles and greetings were exchanged,
Some were young and some had aged,
And some just babes
But they were all known to me,
And then a man appeared
dressed in white,
He came over
And said, "You leave tonight."
I was perplexed
I thought I'd just arrived,
He took my arm and guided me to a window
Where he showed me a scene
And through the clouds
I saw a woman with the prettiest eyes of green
"She's waiting for you,"
"And that man is your Dad,"
He added, pointing to a man playing a piano,
And I cried because I thought they were dead!
I saw a boy with a dog,
My beloved big brother,
And then I understood,
The woman with him was
my dear sweet mother,
Then I realised why they were absent from this place,
He bade me bid farewell to the present company and

showed me a door,
I felt sad for I thought I would see them no more,
But he touched me on the shoulder,
"You will meet them again, like you have before."
It occurred to me that these were friends of the soul
And they would be wherever I would go
He whispered to me before I left,
"Protection on your journey,"
Bestowing a blessing on my head,
"You will return, you still have much to learn."
And so I turned to depart,
To follow my destiny
To follow my heart
For this wasn't the end, it was just the start.

My guardian grandad

I found some photos from long ago,
My grandfather - James John Campbell,
Affectionately "Jock"
Posing for the camera
In a by gone era,
A pilot in the war,
Far from home
Putting on a brave face
While his wife and babies
Prayed and waited
For his return,
I knew his love and kindness
As a child,
I came as a late blessing
in the autumn of his years,
Following him around in my dungarees,
We fed the chickens and ducks
And stopped to pass the time of day with Jason,
Now Jason was destined for the pot,
But Grandad could never bring himself to send the sheep to slaughter,
And Jason lived out his days in happy harmony with the hens,
Neither could he put an end to the poultry,
So soft was his heart,
That was Gran's job,
Rusty, the pointer, would wait for us to appear so we could
survey the plot,
Grandad and me in the early morning sunshine,
Was anyone stealing mangoes?
Were the veggies being watered?

And we kept the slugs and snails away from the
Chrysanthemums,
Or all hell would break loose from Gran;
He lived for church and the way to his heart was to sit beside
him every Sunday
And I tried with all of mine not to fall asleep on his comfortable
shoulder during service,
Sweets were doled out to all the children of the pious
From his bottomless pockets,
As Gran and I waited at the church steps
Wanting our Sunday roast,
And away we would speed
Dorothy clinging on for grim death as Grandad rode the clutch
all the way home,
Dorothy stands on my book case eying me suspiciously now,
She travelled everywhere with Grandad,
This little Zulu relic from his Durban days,
I pray she doesn't move
For when she falls, I know something is wrong,
Like the day my cousin Beverly perished in an accident,
Dorothy fell three times,
Eventually I stopped and said, "Okay, Grandad, what are you
trying to tell me?"
Then I got the news.
It was always his job to break bad news,
Like the day he rang me in tears to tell me my youngest aunt
had left us.
How I miss you, Grandad.
You always gave us blessings when we were ill,
Baptised me when I was eight,
And prayed for my brother every time he returned to the bush,

another young soldier far from home,
If you were here now you would take my hand and say,
"Heavenly Father will provide."
He watches over me from above,
Of this I am sure,
This comforts me much
And just some days I need to know this more than others.

The old bedroom

I passed through our old bedroom today
The first bedroom we lay together in, in England
And the watercolours still hung on the walls
And the curtains that enveloped us were still draped around the bed,
The little window held the same aspect
Just like today when the sky is grey,
And I was reminded of the autumn we spent
In that room
Still navigating our new surroundings
And finding our feet in a strange and foreign place
Our lives in Africa not quite forgotten
Still coming back to us in our dreams
Where our daughter clung to my breast to find some comfort
Feeding off our stress and confusion
And where the boys lay in their downstairs bedroom
Bewildered by the loss of everything they had known,
How eerie was that space?
Where the ghosts of our former selves dwell in the shadows and
light places,
A family torn apart from longing
No longer belonging,
An ill fit,
My heart was wrenched from me
Wandering those rooms today in the late afternoon,
Although with the art appreciation group,
My thoughts were not with the paintings
But with us,
The former us,
The way we used to be

The way we could no longer be
The arguments and fights
We poured into the ears of the children,
In a lifetime sixteen years ago
Another life, another day
A different time
Not us now
Although I am still me,
Everyone else
Everything else
Has gone,
I do not want to return to that house
Where we lived and cried
And slowly
Bit by bit fell apart
Disintegrated,
I will leave it in the stilted air,
In the settling dust.

5

Other Horizons

Dreams of sand

I want to feel sandals in Sahara sand
Wear bright and baggy culottes
Eat oranges from my lover's hand
Sip mint green tea from silver pots on a Moroccan rooftop terrace
Lose myself in a mosaic of Marrakesh tiles
Gaze into the distance and see a vista of colourful doorways
Ride on a camel
Sleep under the stars in a Bedouin tent
Breathe in the spices of the *souks*
Run with you into our dreamed adventure
Absorb and bathe in the blinding sun of a North African morning
Feel the terrified excitement of the snakes and the monkeys
and madness,
Eat from the exotic dish of life
And pretend we could live like this forever

Thoughts from abroad

I've walked in the walled city
Seen the tombs of the dead
Explored the wonders of lost civilisations
Pondered on their lives, their loves, their secrets,
Their passions hidden in the seals of stone
Followed you through dark passages
And holy shrines
Shuddered in the shadows as spirits brushed passed,
Had that moment of panic in the gloom
entering the barely lit chambers
where there is a sense that time is suspended in the dust;
Then I remembered who was beside me
and forward we moved into the light
marvelling at the precise symmetry of the tiles
Listening to unfathomable tongues in the market
Haggling, bargaining, pleading for that unaffordable artefact,
A little memento of a shared holiday in the sun.

40 degrees in Marrakesh

Today I passed through the gates of Hades itself
Walked and walked until my flagging body could endure no more
and still we continued on,
The oppressive heat squeezing it's burning grip around my
forehead and holding it fast till I felt my eyeballs might burst,
I stood on the square and felt the wave of the furnace breathe
into my very spirit,
Boiling the contents of my brain
A pot of tripe on the stove,
Perspiration pouring out of every pore
Of my burnished skin,
Till I felt like a ripe red tomato splitting in a skillet of hot oil,
My feet swollen, hot, lethargic
All feeling gone
My fingers blown up to twice their size
Many times I felt faint
Many times I faltered
And at one point giving up the will to go on
At my lowest, strangers offered charity
A comfortable cushion
A seat in a dark, cool passage
Encouraging glances
For hospitality and charity are given freely in these parts,
Drunk on delirium I called out for my mother
She cannot come
She's been six years gone
Never in all my years have I felt the like.
The heat, the stink, the animals on the brink of starvation
and desperation

I heard the call to prayer
The square around the mosque almost empty
The men gone to give devotion
Drained from the fast, the thirst, the heat
I was too tormented by my own lot
To worry about their suffering:
Now I rest
The ordeal over
Nothing could entice me back to the medina
It has been an experience I will not repeat.

In the shadow of the mosque we wandered

Under the palms in the night
And the children hung from the walls
And horses and the calèches waited
Their smell thick in the air,
The scooters parked in the side street
And they answered the call from everywhere,
The Imam's voice booming over the city
Mesmeric we moved in the direction
Like the snakes in the square
Powerless to resist
Following too
Though not of this faith;
Man upon man gathered
In robes of white outside,
The devoted
Drunk from worship
Bodies weak from the fast
Spirits unwavering
An English parson would be green with envy at this congregation
As we were filled with awe
And we watched, moved at the sight.

Marrakesh 13th June 2016

Seven days in Marrakesh
(For Vince)

When I look back on that holiday
I remember it with great fondness.
For me it was more than an adventure
More than my first holiday abroad
It was an awakening
A new dawn
A retracing of youth
A sudden feeling of being alive
A breath of life after a long borne winter
That had lasted many years
And dragged me down
More than I had realised.
And then your delicious suggestion
to take off and go
To open cloudless skies
Well, it was something I couldn't resist.
Well-worn sandal type of weather
Panama hats and kaftans
Riding through the palm grove on camels called Aisha and
Sophia,
Holding on for grim death as the taxi drivers
Went helter-skelter through the craziness of the backwards traffic
Belting under impossibly narrow arches
Saying secret prayers that no one else
was beating a haste in the opposite direction,
Beautiful stray cats and dogs we wanted to take home.
Your sister's tears at the treatment of the donkeys with their
impossible burdens,

The tiles, the colours, the lamps and carpets.
And beyond the outer walls of the city
Some of the sights we saw,
The funny ladies on scooters with all their children balancing
behind them
And the man who had a sheep on the back of his,
Cattle upstairs on a double decker bus
The goats sitting in a tree
And the mystery of how they got up there
A bus load of foreign tourists and a driver would couldn't speak
our language
Road signs in Arabic and French
Not knowing where we were in the vast expanse of a land
unfamiliar
And the sheer exhilaration of the feeling
We might actually be lost and never found.
The contrast of arid land and lush gardens sitting side by side
The bounty of vegetables and fruit grown in the desert
The kindness of strangers
The generosity of the poor,
The day you took me to the gardens
And how we posed for photos for our social media walls
So our friends could trace our journey.
Nights on the veranda
Gin and tonic, funny cigarettes
Sharing the festivities with the hotel staff
Given a temporary reprieve from the rigorous fasting
As the sun slipped down over the mountains.
The laughter, the friendship, the fun
The afternoons by the pool,
Plumbago and jacaranda

Fish bowls and all-over massages,
Rooftop garden luncheons
Late night conversations
And the friends we made along the way
I thank you for all that.
But for more than that
For understanding why I needed that holiday
For being the friend who offered it.
It takes one who has been on a similar path
To appreciate the sentiment
And for that reason
I will always treasure the memory of those sun-filled days
And now when the weather is upon our heads
Grey and gloomy under a watery sky,
I will smile and remember
your open-hearted kindness.

Wedding in Mijas

(For Mi Amiga Rosa and Jo)

The bride wore navy blue and the groom was suited and booted too
Surrounded by their grown up children,
A hundred silver balloons floated up to the ceiling
Adding to the light and jolly feeling
To the delight of the grandchildren watching in wide eyed
wonderment.
When the couple spoke their vows standing face to face
We saw the love in their eyes and felt the commitment of their promise
And although we didn't understand it
we shed happy tears for our friends
Moved by the emotion of the occasion.
We joined in with the family wishing them well
Posed for photographs under the arch of flowers
Felt a sense of honour to be included
being welcomed, feed and watered
Given every possible care
Nothing was missed in this open hearted hospitality
The wine flowed and the food was plentiful
And we gave thanks and basked in the light of friendship
And we dance the flamenco
And Jo gave it a go
With the pasodoble
And was admired and loved and taken into their hearts
This beautiful and gregarious woman
Who found a lifelong friend in a stranger
Who happened to cross her path
And she was given an open invitation to future parties.
I smiled and stumbled through broken Spanish

My tongue trying on new words
And they applauded my efforts and gave gentle encouragement
And although we spoke a different mother tongue
Somehow we managed to communicate
Somehow we were in perfect concord
And as the night grew late
We shared the time together
Totally letting go,
And when we wandered back
Weary to our beds in the small hours of the morning
Our hearts were full
And our souls were happy
And on returning to our frosty land
To once more scrap the ice from the windscreen
We will look back and remember
that weekend in Màlaga
And keep it somewhere special
To treasure and to never forget
That friends can be found when we least expect them.

The lone saxophonist of Mykonos

As we strolled along the front
Between Old Port and Little Venice
We caught the music wafting on the breath of the breeze
While he stood in the shadows playing out to the sea
Caressing his saxophone with so tender a touch
Coaxing out her lamentable tune,
Memories bitter sweet
To ones once loved
And to his heart left so far across the water
The melancholic melody
Mixing with the tears
of the incoming tide,
And we too were filled to the brim
With feeling,
So moved were we by his song.

With love from Mykonos

The sun has arrived like a warm friend
To fend the wind
And wrap us in its love,
Like two arch enemies
They compete
Good and evil
Kalo kai kako
One a friend
One a foe;
And here on the island
Another day begins
With its slow pace
For there is no hurrying here
It has no significance
In this place of myth and legend
Where history is seeped into the fabric of its being
Where one gets a sense
That civilisation has its roots in this very spot,
So what are we mortals
Compared to the gods?
We can no more control the elements
Than shape the future
That has already been decided
Has already gone before,
Even the air feels timeless
The winds that whip the island
And shift the sand
Teach the lesson
That it is out of our hands

So arise from your beds
Welcome the sun
And the winds that come,
For blessings and tribulations come in equal measure,
Wish your neighbour good day
And as you wander on your way
Leave it to the hands of fate
For what's awaiting you will not come too late
And what's not meant for you
Can never be yours
So leave it now in the lap of the gods
Like this sun blessed isle
It will find you in a while,
Clear the dreams from your fog-filled head,
They are illusions
They have no real quality,
Only to serve as a mirror
To your desire,
Do not invite them to invade your thoughts
Like pirates who plunder your shores of calm
Stand serene
Like this fair isle
And be open to receive
Breathe deep this clean air,
For what you attract will be yours to keep
Be comforted in the knowledge
That you are nurtured
You are protected
You will not be forsaken,
Just go gently
For this is your day.

Travel the world they say

There is educational value in it.
But chose your travelling companions carefully.
Sometimes I sit beside the ocean and let the water lap against my feet,
Lighthouse in the distance
Devonshire green fields at my back,
As I take in the view
And realise how lucky I am.
Then I look across the sea,
And I remember.
Sometimes I see us sitting in a French cafe on the Brittany coast,
Eating buckets of mussels drenched in garlic butter
And remember that glorious day
at Chez Paulette,
The stories and the scenery that washed over us,
Or drinking sangria cocktails in the sunshine with a gorgeous friend,
Whose lust for life is infectious,
Tales of Spanish dancing, shenanigans
Being up all night,
Walking back to the hotel in the rain at 4am
And how we escaped to watch football with the old men in the Italian coffee shop,
I cannot look at a tub of aioli
And not smile.
Beautiful wedding, beautiful embracing Spanish friends.
Then sometimes I return to Morocco
The mystery, the romance, the vibrancy
Seven days of pure escapism

That captured my imagination
When the heat took my breath completely away from me,
And the friend that just brings out the naughty in me.
It has to be said his knack for sailing on the windy side of caution
Is an irresistible drug for one who doesn't take risks.
Or I remember the Irish holidays
Soaking up the heritage and magic of the land
And a desire to return to a time and place
Where my ancestors walked and lived and left
You can feel the pain and history in every corner of that country
It is soaked into it like its rain drenched soil
And yet the people are like family
They welcome you as such
And after five minutes on a bus
You feel like you've always known them
No one is a stranger in Ireland.
I've braved the crossing three times now
And every time has been worth it
Even in a moment of utter madness
When it was attempted between Christmas and New Year
A few years ago
Gale force winds and being as sick as one can be in such conditions
Thank goodness for a caring friend
Who didn't mind me smelling of puke for three days
The sight of the Dunbrody on the river
Was something I can never forget
And the idea that my great, great grandfather sailed to
South Africa in such a vessel, brought me to tears.
They were true adventurers
Intrepid explorers,
And I am grateful to them.

So where will life take us in the new year
As we plan our holidays
Time spent discovering the world is never wasted
Just open that door
Open your mind and just do it.
Happy, safe travels to you all.

From a veranda in Mykonos

(For Darrell)

We sat beside the Aegean
My good friend and I
Looking out across the ocean
Looking out across the sky
And under an expanse of blue
We shared our stories
Old and new,
And made a toast to all that's gone before
And places and faces
We will see no more
And had a look back over a friendship
Of a quarter of a century
And congratulated ourselves on how far we've come
And how we never thought
We'd be sitting here in the sun on this Grecian isle
Toasting and talking in fine style
And in a while
We might well take a stroll to the water's edge
Dip a toe in
And make a pledge
To remember this perfect day
When we're far away
From this beautiful place
And the humdrum of life has returned to its usual pace,
And we'll remember our afternoons on this sun-drenched
veranda
And the blue and white streets
Where we did meander

On that wonderful holiday of a lifetime
When taking a break from his life and mine.
When we sat soaking up that glorious sunshine,
Drinking wine
Till dinner time.

Greek Independence Day
25th March 2019

A priest lead a small procession along the front
And they carried garlands of flowers
And pictures of the Blessed Virgin
To pay homage to the Angel Gabriel
As they walked towards the little church on the edge of the bay
The priest said prayers for those gone away
To the life hereafter,
Heralding in the Annunciation
In the Lenten season,
The children in traditional dress follow the cross
Boys in blue waist coats and white tunics
Girls in red and gold dresses
As the sellers proffer
Flags
To the tourists,
And sitting here on the bench
An interested bystander,
I wonder how many lives were lost
In a population where nearly a third were left standing,
And the soldiers who fought
To give this proud Hellenic nation its freedom
In the days when Ottoman rule
Exercised its influence here,
And as I wait for the service to finish
And for the celebrations to begin
I ponder on how much tenacity it took
To stand up to the might of the Turks
Massacres and atrocities on both sides

Bloodshed, impoverishment, sacrifice;
And on this near prefect day
As I sit and eat my gelato
Almost two hundred years later
I am suddenly struck by my insignificance
And I am truly humbled
As I make my way back to the hotel.

Farewell to this fair Grecian isle

Through Mykonos streets did I meander
Oftentimes losing my way
In the labyrinthine arteries
Of white,
Hearing conversations in a tongue foreign to my ears,
But like sweet honey they flow into my brain
As I learn to comprehend a few precious words,
Local people touching up the walkways with pots of white paint,
Last week there were no tourists,
This week there have been a few,
Asking for directions and like me getting lost,
Muscles aching from the effort of exertion
navigating the narrowing paths of the town,
And in my silent reflection I am shown the churches
In all their simplistic splendour
Pure white
Like our Blessed Virgin,
And hear the bells in high towers calling the faithful
To prayer.
And the most beautiful of all, Paraportiani
Beside the door,
One can only stand and gaze at its brilliance
Where the white dome meets the sky,
Heaven-blessed,
Onward, I catch glimpses of the sea
Through different vistas,
Brilliant shades of blue
So typically Aegean
And I have to stop to take in the view

Breathe in the air
Feel the sun seeping into my bones,
Capture in my mind's eye
The wild spring flowers bursting into brilliant colour
On the sides of outcrops,
Violets and poppies,
Where the winds relentlessly batter the bay
And the windmills stand proud
Like five beautiful daughters
Beckoning their families home
The mimosa trees lining the road into town give a cheery
welcome to travel-weary walkers
Like myself, a lone explorer,
Blissful to have the place to myself
In the out of season month of March,
In the upcoming months it will become too crowded for me
Too loud for my taste
And the all night parties too youthful for my time of life,
I am happy to see the wood sorrel hugging the rocks
That provides a brilliant display for my artistic eye,
And today I must push on
To visit a fellow compatriot of mine, beautiful Donna,
A friend I'd never met till today,
And as our easy conversation
Dispels all awkwardness
We draw in close
as we talk of our old country,
Familiar places and different stages of our lives,
And we share tea and stories on her veranda
and break pieces of halva,
In a place that will soon burst into the purple flowers

of the bougainvillea,
We discuss the frustrations of modern day politics,
Brexit and the senselessness of separation when we belong to
one universal family,
Here in this beautiful corner of the town
Looking down into the streets
Where neighbours pass and greet,
And later she walks me back to the hotel at sunset
And we embrace like old companions
Our ties to Africa completing the circle of friendship,
The invisible threads that bind us
One sister to another;
And so I must face the long journey home
As I leave this island paradise in the Cyclades
Where I arrived a stranger six days hence
But I feel I leave it as a friend,
I am not wracked with sorrow
I am blessed with peace
For I suspect I will return
One of these fine tomorrows,
And until then I will keep this place
And this journey of my soul
Closely tucked inside my heart.

As the weary travellers make their way home

Shaking the dust of a foreign land from their feet

Over indulgent stomachs and flaky skin

From dodgy sun tans

Spider bites and eggs embedded in the skin

Stiff legs, swollen feet, stinging eyes

Plaguing their early hours back in Blighty

Walking from the furnace and into the refreshing rain of another British summer

Looking forward to a proper English breakfast with proper full fat bacon

A Lidstone's sausage roll or Devonshire pasty

A strong cup of Yorkshire tea

Things we take for granted

Things that matter,

They will sigh and think of the holiday abroad

Treasure the bright souvenirs

And remember the happy smiles of the local people in the land of the desert

The Arabic road signs

The exotic plants

The photo of the camel ride

Sun filled days and alcohol fuelled nights

New friends made and promises to return

Resolutions to learn French

Buy a Moroccan cook book

Eat more aubergine

Wear the colourful jalabiyas in the land of grey skies in spite of strange stares,

Yes, it was a grand adventure and now that we have returned
Feeling enriched by the experience
And recalling that blue sky feeling
And being lost and not minding
Happy and drunk and in love with it all
We put our fatigue aside
And travel back to Marrakesh in our dreams.

Travellers

Blessed are they who seek to find,
We are all travellers,
Exiles,
Searchers of the truth,
Discoverers of new lands
Cousins of the world,
We flock together
To find our brothers and sisters
In the lands beyond our own,
Our common thread
Our blood ties,
Forget their insular lies
We are greater than these imposed borders,
Like migratory birds who seek dry land,
We have travelled far
Added to our universal family
And so when we seek new horizons
We find ourselves
In the smiles of strangers
In the hospitality of a welcome
And those who understand
That it is through travelling
You learn what you already knew.
So throw your doors open
Befriend a fellow traveller
The backpacker on the roadside,
For you never know when that person will be you,
Listen to their stories
Add your own,

Learn their language
Even if it's just a few words
It is the greatest compliment
You can give people
To communicate in a common language
And keep reaching to connect
For it is through our connections
That we strive for greater understanding
Greater peace.

6

Inspirational

The people in my head have gone to bed

The people in my head have gone to bed
Thank goodness for that
Leave them there for a while
The cat is asleep on the chair
And so I turn to my thoughts once more, now that I am
completely alone
Watching a myriad of colours bursting into the dark of a cloudy sky
And listening to the parties going on around me
while they toast and cheer and raise a glass to absent friends dear
I will lay ghosts of last year to rest
And send a wish into the night
For peace and solitude
To restore and repair
Detox old emotions to purify the spirit.
For those that I love I ask for
an extra helping of good health and happiness
To be sprinkled all around them
To clothe them in protection and to give fortitude to face another year.
And as I look back on it,
A thousand reflections flood my mind
And I give thanks to everything that came my way
For the laughter shared with special ones
For the love of family
And the moments spent in private contemplation.
For strangers who became friends
And the joy of learning a new language
To the new lands I've travelled to
And for the lovers who live in my dreams
For the kindness and the help freely given

And for the angels who have crossed my path again
I thank you for walking beside me, all those seen and unseen;
To those who offer me guidance when I am flagging and keep me
upright when I'm falling
I am sincerely grateful,
For those who have left us
I send a prayer up for eternal peace for your resting souls
You will be missed and thought of always.
And for those who have experienced loss
A prayer of comfort
for we all
have spiritual families
separated by a thin curtain
In a different dimension
You are not far, it just that we cannot see you.
And so as we put the past behind us
Let's leave it there
Tomorrow dawns a new day
Who knows what it will bring.
Let's embrace it, enjoy it and leap right into it.
It might just be the start of something
enduringly wonderful.

Clear your mind and relax

What battles need to be fought today?
Is it necessary to over-think the situation
And are those people you are churning the troubled waters of
your brain about,
Are they worried about you right now?
Reach into the depths of your belly and take a long, deep breath
Does today belong to you or are you going to let someone else
steal it from you?
Stop for just a moment
Still the voices, stop the doubts
You have been here since the beginning
People have come in one door
And gone out another
Your have survived thus far through your own determined will
And will continue to do so once they have all departed
Do you value their opinion
Or is this just a reaction to their words and actions?
What is the emotional investment in this situation?
Can you get out of it without compromising yourself
and your principles?
Is it going to harm you or harm others?
Does it really matter?
Take a step back
What will work for you at this precise moment?
High blood pressure? A migraine?
Let's take a walk in a forest
Have a warm drink
Give yourself a cuddle and a pat on the back
Well done!!

Here's to everything you've accomplished, and you're still here to tell the tale.
Look up to the sky and forget that worry in your mind.
You could be somewhere else today
Somewhere far better
Anywhere you choose
Forget those people who impinge on your energy,
We have a limited amount of breaths in this lifetime
Make each one count
Breathe it for your enrichment
Live the day for you
This is your life, your moment, your time
Go forth and enjoy!

Never waste a word

Never waste a moment,
For once the opportunity is missed,
It is gone,
If you say something with a pure heart
And give it with good intent,
It doesn't make you a lesser person
If it is not accepted
With the grace with which it was given
For the gift was yours to give.
Not everyone appreciates a pearl
Until it is lost in the sand,
Not everyone appreciates a rainbow
Until it vanishes in the vapour,
So cry not if it is rejected,
For those who cannot see your worth
Will realise only too late
And although you heart is burdened with boundless love
And you feel it has nowhere to go,
You are the richer, my friend,
For in the end
You can never know where the ripples of that stone thrown
Will reach;
You are one of the golden ones,
One of the beautiful souls,
One who comes to love,
One who comes to give,
There is a place for you
With love untold,
In measure you cannot hold,

Maybe not in this lifetime
But in the next.
So be bold,
Say those words
When you feel the need
And do not worry if your seeds fall on stones
There is no shame in trying,
No time for denying
And when you do release the love
Open the valve wide
Even if it doesn't meet its mark,
Believe me when I tell you this,
One day it will return to you.

We tell our stories

We write them down,
Words flow from me to you
And back to me.
Love is an energy of thoughts,
A synergy that binds
One to the other
For we are all connected by an invisible thread,
Unfathomable,
A universal consciousness,
Timeless,
Ageless,
A warmth that draws us close,
As precious as a breath
As wonderful as the spark of life,
An ever-living essence,
Subliminal,
With eyes closed
We take the leap
Speak our minds
And draw another human being close,
Trying to put in words
How we feel,
In the hope that in our yearning to be whole,
To find it's equal half,
In a world where want leads to hunger
We cleave to the one
Who restores us to our centre of calm,
Gravitate to like-minds
Soul companions;

It's simple when you break it down,
Love is all we have to give
All we have to take
Into the next world,
Communication helps us to express this,
Words give meaning to the way our hearts feel,
Intellect is at the very core of every soul
And it will lead us out of ignorance and into the light
When our time comes,
We can say we are truly enlightened,
Just like a river cannot resist
Flowing into the sea
Neither can we resist this life force,
We must express!
A poet uses words, as an artist uses paint,
A pen to a brush
So let peace descend,
Everything you need you already have,
And let the tide of warmth and words and feeling
rush over you
Let it spill over,
For it flows from you
to me,
In an everlasting sea.

Wrong turns can be the best turns

Do not measure the path of your life in chronological years
Mark it in memories and moments
And the magnificence and magnitude of it all.
When you take a wrong turn
And you are lead to somewhere other than where you imagined,
Let your spirit breathe in the view
And rejoice in delight.
When a small act of kindness
Changes the course of your life
Setting you on a path you never imagined
Remember things happen for reason
Enjoy this moment now
Pick up where you left off
And just escape.
Climb on a gate in the wide open space
And let your legs just dangle
Take off your shoes and wade through the water
Let your body shiver and come alive in a refreshing, cold stream
Reflect, rejuvenate and restore
Surround yourself with the colours you love
Listen to the early morning birds
Throw open the window and let in the possibilities.
Play that tune that makes your heart sing
And fill your voice with song.
This is your life
Who cares if anyone is listening?
Dance if it makes you feel good
Run if you can
Feel the sand under your toes

And the sun on your skin
If you care for someone
Pick up that phone and make it right
For we never know when it will be too late.
Love your friends, avoid your enemies
And should someone harm you
With a sharp and cruel word
Remember it is nothing to do with you
Don't react to their ugliness.
You are above that.
Yes, you are soaring in the sky
with those birds and that red and blue kite.
Do not judge yourself by anyone else's standards
They don't wear your shoes
And they have had a different journey.
Let you mind be the camera that captures your happy times
Let your heart hold in it everything that matters to you
Say yes to all the invitations
Say no to things and people who steal your precious time
Think of this way
We have limited time here
don't waste a second on someone else's priorities
Just so that you can be ticked off to their "to do" list
If they rely on you so much
They should treat you better.
Look after yourself first.
The clock will tick on no matter what we do
There's no stopping it.
So don't waste a moment
Go and do it now.

Thoughts at three

I'm not unhappy with my lot in life
Most journeys are made for a reason
So as I steady the pen in the wee small hours
While my neighbours are away to their slumbers
I slip into my reflections
A life lead in the service of others;
Childhood dependency of two children
Twelve years apart;
The wants and needs of a spouse;
The children are grown ups now
And a mother's duty seems redundant;
As for the other
The charade seemed pointless after nearly thirty years,
Wasted years in the landscape of regret and recrimination
So I departed grabbing what was left of life
while I was still young enough to enjoy it.
When there's nothing to say
Silence is the only answer.
It's just me and the cat now
She isn't mine but has moved in
And glad I am to have her
Solitude is more bearable with company.
As far as love goes
I am neither hopeful nor cynical
Content for the time being to be on my own,
Keeping my own council.
But I keep the dream alive
Being, as my friends call me 'a hopeless romantic'
Hopeless – because I am always searching

For that one, true, perfect love
That falls wide of the mark.
And romantic because I still believe it's out there somewhere.
For now I see it as another four letter word
Like pain, lust, want and need.
If it does exist, it will have to find me.
And even when it does come knocking
It may well find me hiding under the bed
Till it goes away.
As for this time of the year
I am not keen
Wet winters play havoc with my sinus
The cold makes my joints creaky
Then there are the days when the migraines are upon me
Time to block out the light and retreat into my cave.
These are the worst
When I feel most desperate and alone
They have become very severe of late
My head on a knife point of pain
Eyes feel like they've been scooped out with a melon spoon.
The green queasy feeling taking over my belly
Days of my life lost in the darkness till it passes.
Work appears to be my opium when I am on top form.
I occupy my days until exhaustion sets in and then I must retreat
into my world of silence.
I must find a better balance
But it keeps me sane and my complaints are few
And while there is still energy in this body
I will live to face another day
For what else can I do?

As we look forward to the New Year

The time has come, my friends, to think about the future
So whilst you're holding hands and singing Auld Lang Syne
Toasting absent friends
and making resolutions
I wonder what you will wish for yourself?
What will you wish for others?
Once the party is over
And the hangovers too
as we pass New Year's Day groaning on the sofa
What then?
I suppose the question we have to ask ourselves is ...
What makes us truly happy,
Prosperity?
Can the pursuit of wealth really buy happiness?
We need some of it to keep the wolf away from the door, this is
for certain,
But if you spend all your time
Surrounding yourself with material things
And forget that sometimes
The most valuable commodity is time
Then what will you have?
To give someone your undivided attention
Is probably the best present,
Just kicking back and having a laugh with someone you care for
is a tonic you can both share.
Good health is always a good thing to wish for yourself and
others
So perhaps it's time to review our habits
Small steps every day

This will definitely help
Without being too fanatical.
Peace is another good wish to pass on to friends and family
We all need a bit of that in this manic life we lead.
Sadly consideration and empathy
For others seems to have gone out of the window
In this "all about me" life,
Where we are the star of our own show.
Time to put our egos on the shelf perhaps
Others are entitled to shine too
To have their say,
Their opinions
We don't always get it right
But isn't part of the joy of life sharing
Each other's little victories
And being there with a listening ear
And a cup of tea when people have disappointments.
I pray that I will be more open to that
In the coming months
And not be so obsessed with my own concerns.
For me, Love is a big one and something I would wish for someone
It is selfless and beautiful,
There's no enough of that, in my opinion!
So dear hearts, as you get ready for your parties in the next few days
I thank you for your support and kindness
And for the friendships I've made on this medium,
I wish you all happiness, love, peace and good health
With a little sprinkling of wealth
Just enough for you to share
To show you care

As we leave the last year behind
Let's pray the new one will be kind
So pull your loved ones near
Show them that they are dear
And tell them you love them
For when we are no longer here
That's all that will matter.

The poet at Christmas 2017

The poet at Christmas was pondering her life
What a year this had turned out to be,
Joy and elation,
With the blessing of a new life
For a beloved son and his beautiful wife,
Holding the precious baby for the first time
And the love that passed between them.
What could be better than a first grandchild?
In the silence of the moment
The poet thought of another victory
Liberation from trouble and strife
Release from emotional imprisonment
The final withering away of something
that had caused much distress,
No use thinking about
that abysmal relationship.
And in her home country
a despicable dictator deposed
Bringing healing like the lancing of a horrible abscess.
Betrayal, drama and intrigue
Overwork, migraines and fatigue,
And the determination to distance one's self from it.
The contentment that comes from the knowledge that you don't
need one bit of it!
That you have all that you need.
Everything is under control
There's not a thing that happens in this life that wasn't planned,
Ordained
Predestined

Patience is the only key that unlocks the door
And the poet smiled to herself
For no one else was in the room
Apart from the sleeping cat,
There is no need to fight it
No reason to have all the answers
And no need to waste another minute of her time
On the accumulation of things
And words that didn't rhyme,
Or wasted emotions on people unworthy
Of her affection
For when she loved she did it with all her heart,
Those who wanted to be in her life already were
And she was much comforted
By the company of her own presence
She was on her own
But she wasn't alone
For those seen and unseen
Were in her heart
And were warming it on this wet and damp Christmas Eve.
And so to the future ...
For our poet, is a forward thinker
Yes, there will challenges
And some lean days ahead
But just over yonder
Freedom is waiting
like the little spring seeds
That are already germinating.
But as it is Christmas after all
The burden will not be shouldered today
And snuggling into her warm crochet blanket

She set aside these ponderings
And basked in the glow of the occasion
Offering up a prayer of thanks
A prayer of protection for the most beloveds
At this time of peaceful reflection.

It's the last day of the year

It's the last day of the year
And I'm as fat as a fig
Fit to burst
And I wasn't even that overly indulgent
this festive season,
For this very reason!
Nonetheless no one will want to get jiggy
with this little piggy,
So something will have to be done
But now is not the time to be dieting
With the flu bugs rioting
Best to keep the immune system strong
And you can't go wrong,
But I'll jump onto the scales for a bit of giggle
And with a twist and a wiggle
I am able to see the figures
Oh my giddy Aunt and Uncle!
This is definitely diabolical
Perhaps a measure of belt tightening
And modicum of moderation
Might need serious consideration
If I want to return to a vague representation
Of an hour glass
Something will have to be done about this …
And fast!
I'd put the Christmas chocs in the bin
But they're already gone
I've managed to turn down offers of three Christmas cakes
And mince pies a plenty

My dresses are getting somewhat tenty
Meal planning and a healthy recipe
Are now a necessity.
So out with the old
And in with the new
For what else am I to do
If I want to stand half a chance
Of a date
Surely it's not too late
Let's crack on
Avaunt spare tyre
Be gone!
And roll on summer
And here's to my new lover
Whoever that might be!

Rise above the mundane

I'd like to rise above the mundane and just for once think about
something more urbane
And forget that my job is hanging by a thread
In spite of what employment law has said
And that it doesn't matter that I'm struggling to make ends meet
And I haven't got comfortable shoes on my feet,
And that I'm still paying for heating
Even though it's Spring but the sun is retreating
And that I am drunk with fatigue
But I still have mouths to feed
And that paying off my debt
Is something that causes me to fret
And that maintenance payments are bringing me to my knees
For a child that the parent never sees,
And I want forget that my love life is non-existent
And the silliness of it all seems persistent,
And that government is extreme
Democracy is now a far off dream
And that no one wants to take the blame
And every day it's a losing game
And that we are constantly bombarded by horrible news
And that politicians are in constant stews
Scandals and denials
New data protection and missing files,
Brexit is just not a funny joke
And I think we've been lumbered with a pig in a poke
And that plastic is polluting the ocean
And the state of the world is in perpetual motion,
Quite frankly it's all gone to pot

As we sink deeper into the rot
And the Tories lead the working classes down the garden path
And the fact that Donald Trump is visiting just a laugh
I'm finding it hard to be positive about anything
I mean come on, how long is a ball of string?
I can't see the woods for the trees
And now it's the bees
What happens when they disappear from the planet
We'll all disappear, god dammit,
The world's gone quite mad
And it makes me feel very sad
As we drown in paperwork and risk assessments
As slowly down the drain go the investments
And our pensions are worthless
And I'll be working till I'm toothless
Come on now, HMRS don't be ruthless
Surely it's time someone cut us a break
For goodness sake!!
I'll think I'll go and lie in a darkened room
While I contemplate the impending doom
And drown my sorrows in what might have beens
And try to forget what I've seen
And refuse to listen to the News
And all the experts' ghastly views
And pray that tomorrow is not just another wasted day
Where the rain calls off play.
I don't like this game
It's just too boring and always the same
There just isn't any let up
I'm tired of being a grown up
I'm going to just sit on the gate

Make daisy chains and just wait,
Maybe Mum will call me into tea
Just like it used to be.

In my heart

I have kept many things
For I find it difficult to let them go,
Half a century of things I have treasured,
I have hidden,
All my joys,
All my sadness,
Memories,
Some best forgotten
Some I will cherish forever,
And now I feel
I need to make room
Clear some space
For I am over-burdened by it all,
And so I think I will have to sift
And painfully sort
And decide what to keep
And what to discard,
The unhappy childhood can go for a start,
But how do I throw this out
Without losing my nucleus?
The very atoms that made me?
Their failings were my torture.
Their decisions impacted on my young life,
I guess they never realised
How a sensitive child can suffer.
I'll also take out the disappointing romances
And just keep the good ones,
But wouldn't that be impossible,
For aren't there good days

And bad days in any relationship?
And if I rid myself of these
What about my most treasured ones,
Who would never have been born,
Had I not stumbled across those who broke my heart?
I am soaked through with sorrow
I am lame from carrying this heavy bag,
Alone now
I must wade through it
Or sink under it,
And so if I am to survive
I must rise above and
Empty the vessel,
And fill it with everything
That feeds my spirit,
For there will be others to replace the gaps,
And as we move slowly and yet surely towards the end,
It's best to get things into perspective
We are not redundant just because our dear ones have left the nest,
And the failed romances are not necessarily a reflection on us,
If it proves one thing, it's that we love too much
The problem is when we expect the same from others
And when it doesn't materialise,
Disappointment sets in,
So to guard against future hurt
Against future pain,
We must be very wise
Weigh things up,
For we will love again,
We will trust again,
It's just a matter of time.

In the company of trees

When your spirit is heavy with concern
Take yourself off to the wooded paths
Away from the busyness of life
Lean on nature for a bit,
Let the quiet offer you cooling balm
And just enjoy the calm,
Stand in the middle of the trees
And let the serene green
Be a comforting womb,
This is where mankind was born,
This is our original home.
Stretch your arms up
And emulate the branches
Reaching for the sky
Feel your soul earthing
With the soil
And the twisted, moss covered roots,
Sit for a while and clear your mind
Listen to the birds above the canopy of the leaves,
Let their song sooth you,
Feel the strength in the trunk of a tree
And it's stoic indifference
To the human ants bustling about it
on the motorway in the distance,
And if you are very still
You might catch the squirrels at play
And notice the hazel pregnant with nuts
Or the fine thin fingers of the angelica on the edges of the forest,
Close your eyes and feel the natural world wrap around you,

And take your lesson therein
Though you be weighted by your troubles
Don't forget to breathe
Don't forget this is your life too
And always take time to escape to the woods
To keep company with the trees.

Someone sent me a heart today

I found it outside when I opened my window,
Lying among the stones
All alone
This little sign
Telling me that love is on its way,
I wouldn't have noticed it
But today, being a Sunday,
I decided to take it slow
It's amazing what you see when you shift down the gears
And maybe this is what I needed to be shown
That it's time to stop rushing,
To stop pushing
Because love arrives when it's ready,
When you are ready,
And it's found in the most secluded places
In unknown faces
And when you least expect it
And most of the time
It happens when you nurture your own heart,
Because it's only when you take time to self-care
That you can dare
To give it back.
And so dear friends,
Look after that one person
Who is always there,
And take time to do what makes you happy
What makes you strong
For the time we have is not long
And it would be wrong

To put other things in first place.
Imagine if you realised today was your last
It would be terrible to have wasted the past
On things that don't really matter,
This really is our last chance,
So start it now
And just do what you've always wanted to do,
People will come and go,
But don't forget about you!

Blow out the candle and come to bed

For tonight we must draw close together
The solstice is upon us
And as the darkness stretches its fingers into the room
And we face the night off spells and wonder
Look into your heart,
As I will look into mine
And let us see what we can find
I'll tell you a secret but you must promise to keep it and never tell
A living soul
For shadows grow among the embers
And there are enemies amongst us
Disguised as friends,
And bide here beside me
for I am afraid to be alone
And as this year draws to an end
Let's be thankful for coming through
for it has been turbulent indeed,
And the power is shifting
like desert sands moving under our feet,
Brother against brother,
We are witnessing the ending of time
For it seems to me the days of this year
Have moved too quickly
It seems like yesterday it was January
And now we are putting this twelve month behind us
And these 366 days are all but spent
So come a little closer,
Your nearness gives comfort
And I will not fret

And should I awake in the night
Just hush me back to sleep
And shelter me from the bad dreams
For what care I if you are here
And what is a long winters eve
When I have the promise of summer in the warmth in your body
And in the morning we will not remember the fear
But embrace the light
And forget that tonight was the longest night.

They say you shouldn't dwell in the past

It's not good for you.
Live in the present,
In the here and now
Live for today.
For me, visiting the past cleanses my soul
And I do it often.
Gives me great solace,
The past has been a kind friend
A friend who walks beside me
A friend who has taught me valuable lessons
And who reminds me how far I've come
And the people who have helped me,
And we should never forget where we're from.
She is a tattoo on my back
I know she's there but I can't always see her.
Another friend, the future
Also walks beside me
She encourages me to look forward
To remember my goal and aspirations
And reminds me that this is all temporary,
And tells me every day
That I am better than this
Better than those who try to put me down
Better than my present struggles,
And that there's more to come, wonderful, beautiful beginnings.
She is tattooed on my heart.
And the last of my friends is the present,
She pulls the curtain on every new day
Says "Come on, let's do it!"

She looks me in the mirror
Every morning and says "Now, then what do you need today?"
She drags me from my bed
And helps me face it.
She's lives in my head,
Reminds me of the gifts I have received recently,
And says today is another day.
And so I introduce you to my three friends
Each one plays a part.
For without the past how can I navigate the future,
And without the present, how can I appreciate the past?
I welcome them into my home
For I am never alone
And on this journey they tag along
And tell me I am strong
For I have endured and still I stand upright
and continue to walk.
So this advice I offer you
Never regret your past,
Appreciate each new day
And always look to the future
For they belong to you
And only you.

I won't let booze numb the pain

Nor take tablets
For me there is no gain.
This is raw, this is real
I feel it in all its gruesome glory,
Embrace it and remember.
It is not for me to deny.
And these tears
I would rather cry
They have made me stronger
Helped me to fight harder,
And if that makes me a weakling
In the eyes of some
It matters not
For I have never been ashamed of who I am.
I've spent years stepping over broken glass
Avoiding the shards, have my feet cut a few times
Been rushed to A&E
Been patched up
I'm not giving anyone that power any more.
Every time it comes crashing down
I've taken the blame
To keep the peace
Now that peace belongs to me
It has been hard won.
There's power in absolute silence,
And as my heart lets out a sigh
The burden is lifted.
My soul is at rest
These little wars we create are only a little light drama

They lessen our value
Shorten our years.
I've taken a step back
I will occupy the front seat no more.
The position of quiet observer is one I now relish.
My years in the spotlight are over.
Let's see how it plays out.
There once was a time
I'd have rushed to be there
Now an early night and the blessing of peaceful restorative sleep
is all I crave.
I sit and quietly congratulate myself
Every time I am proved right.
It gives great satisfaction
Some compensation for the years
I was told I was wrong.
To be born with wisdom can be a curse
In a world that exists only for itself.
Intuition is seen as hocus pocus
But for me it is my passport
I never leave home without it.
To be yourself when everyone else is trying to be someone else
takes a bit of courage.
But until you can do that
Your inner self will never be at peace
You will never find your way home.
So, fly away, find your wings
Loneliness is only a state of mind
And that hand you seek in the dark
may just well turn out to be your own.

Oh, how temporary is the beauty of the moment

When even the blossoms of the cherry
Must fade and die,
Just one week gazing at the wonderful sight and then like confetti
scattered at a wedding, all is gone to the wind:
Even the apple's sweet fragrance must give way to the headiness of
rotting fruit.
How very sad it is to think
spring blooms that force through the earth's cold crust with such
cheery countenances, will give such a glorious golden show for
a week or two
And then crumble to broken and drab decay.
Deep in the woods where carpets of blue adorn hidden pathways
and fairies' bells guide our way
So that we hasten to their shadowy green corners in April to enjoy
the spectacle
But its grace has a limited date
And must be given over before May is out
And when the melody is all but done.
Then June returns full of promise and hope but soon her glory is
but a memory
And the roses we loved so much are petals falling.
And now with July in tow
I see the flowers drooping in the sun
Leaves burning from the heat
And us mere mortals are lethargic from the muggy oppressive
humidity
As we wander around half clad feeling brain-dead by lunch time.
How we complain about the damp cold winters and

long for the summer
But here it is
And there we are midway through and dying for the arrival of
autumn.
I am happy as Larry to see blue skies,
But when the rain came down two weeks ago I threw open the
window and drank in it's refreshing breath.
It just lifted the lid on this heatwave
And I was glad to see it!
The estuary washed in colours of blue and fresh green
paint the scene each day on my way across the bridge,
As the day comes to a close on the golden fields close by;
My goodness, England is beautiful in the summer!
Tomorrow I must trundle up to the moors
And capture them in my inward eye
Now at their best
For soon it will be too cold, too wet and I shall be too miserable!
What a sorry breed we make, us human beings
Are we ever really happy?
Or am I now too English and therefore I must complain about
the weather even when it's thus beautiful?

Freedom

I will no longer be shackled by the chains of the past
For freedom has come at last
And I welcome it!
My heart is an open book
An empty page...
And the pen is poised
To write the next verse,
And how light I feel
As the weight falls away
And although I feel the sunshine in my tired eyes,
I can sleep and dream with ease,
With a clear vision
As the mists lift
To a clear, clean day
Seeing the light's reflection
On the inner windows of my mind's eye
Knowing what's coming next
Is going to be the best,
I am proud to stand alone,
I have paid for the privilege
I welcome new possibilities
Like the ebb and flow of the tide
As I dip my feet in calmer water,
And I bid farewell to the ties
of yesterday,
And as for those lead balloons that have kept me tethered to the
worries of recent years,
I snip the rope
And allow my fears to dissipate

As I send them up into the clouds
And as the fortress falls away
And my vista becomes wider,
Endless,
Unhampered
I hear life's symphony
Soothing my weary spirit
I have walked many paths
Some I should not have ventured onto,
And the mistakes I have made
And the detours taken
Have sent me valuable lessons,
And the friction they have caused
The battles in my tortured mind
Have made the scars
Seen and unseen,
Some I could have done without
I would have chosen an easier journey,
And now as I abandon the walking boots I have worn for so long
I sooth the hard callouses
On these careworn feet of mine
And reach for softer soles
More comfortable chairs
More comforting company,
But now I am older
My lessons have been learnt
I would be content for no more,
And as I move forward
I do so carrying hope
And the belief that anything can happen
For those thoughts we have thrown out into vast void will beam

into the universe,
And we can never know
the full extent of their reach,
And what forces are at play
On our road to our ultimate destiny,
The only thing we can do is trust
For what will be will be,
And with all the best will in the world
It is not in our power to change one iota
of the master plan.
Take comfort
Like I have
For we are not the ones in control, as we may think.

There are some days

There are some days you can do without,
Some days when you want to scream and shout
With frustration
When you're sick and tired
of castigation,
Insinuation,
The same old awful situation,
Days when all you want to do is pack it in
Throw it all up and start again
Far away, in a place where no one knows you,
Days when you could just escape
Miles from the daily grind
Just disappear and hide,
Say to heck with this!
Quite frankly you're taking the …
…Michael
And this existence is frightful!
One problem after another
As we lurch from one crisis to the next
Where is the life I deserve?
This is nonsense
You've really got a nerve!
Where's all the fun?
Where has it gone?
Honestly, I wish they would all take a flying leap
And let me get some sleep
Before I go completely insane
And get a pounding pain in my brain
What more do you want from me?

A pound of flesh?
We are supposed to be grownups
This isn't a crèche!
There are days when you believe you simply cannot go on
And you just want to be gone
Sail away
And just forget about today
And just when you're about to throw in the towel
Stand on a cliff face and just howl,
Then a friend sends you a text
And says you're the best
And that you look amazing
In something or other
And suddenly those doubts that threaten to smother
And pull you under
Disappear
And all at once
hope erases the fear
The sunshine appears
And balance is restored
By just one little act of kindness
From someone you adored!

The butterfly and the bumble bee

For Di

(An Ode to Friendship)

There once was a butterfly
Who was so beautiful
But she hid in the flowers
Cleverly camouflaging her brilliance
For she never knew how lovely she was.
She watched shyly in amongst the petals
Now, on the other side of the garden
There was a bumble bee
Busily working away gathering pollen
The butterfly loved the bumble bee for they were friends
The bee knew the butterfly was sensitive
But she could not help being honest,
And sometimes the butterfly would feel the sting of her words,
She was a romantic soul you see,
And to her, the world would always be a beautiful place
Like this garden in the summertime,
But the butterfly had one little flaw
She found the truth terrifying
She danced around it
Rather than tell the bumble bee how she really felt,
This drove the bee to distraction being a practical sort of creature,
And try as she might
The butterfly could not help
But disguise her feelings in poetic verse,
Then one day the bumble bee told her she was beautiful
And this surprised her because she always thought the bee was
the beautiful and clever one,

The butterfly realised she could not survive without her friend,
For we all need a true friend
And the bumble bee explained that they both served the
same purpose
And there was room for them both to live among the flowers,
But honesty was important in any friendship.
Harmony has been restored to the garden
And although the butterfly is still afraid of her feelings
She is getting braver every day,
For honesty always is
the best policy.

Sitting on the step

I'm just sitting on the step
Watching the world go by
Fruit smoothie in hand
At the start of this beautiful day,
Unravelling my braids,
Kicking off my slippers
Breathing in the pure air,
Listening to the stream
Trickling passed my door,
The sun bronzing my skin
Warming my soul,
As my neighbours rush by to their various occupations,
She joins me,
My little cat,
Leaps onto my lap,
A kind friend offers me a chair
But I'm content on my pile of cushions
In my little bohemian pose,
Writing poetry
Thinking my thoughts
Making my plans,
The laundry needs doing,
Things need completing for work
And I haven't made my bed
I'm not ready yet,
Holding on to this precious moment for as long as I can,
French melodies fill my head
As I drift away
Enjoying the elixir of life

This beautiful early morning sunshine
Before the busyness of the day
Takes me away
To where I'd rather not be,
Let's put that to one side for the moment
And just relish the peace and quiet,
For I have it all here,
My own little haven,
The door open to opportunity
this is what I'm craving,
Even if my dreams and schemes fall into my lap
All I want is mine at this precise moment,
Because it's the simple pleasures of life,
That make you happy and carefree
So here we are,
Away from all the schlep
Just the cat and I sitting on the step.

Painting fields yellow

I'd like to disappear for a while
Leave the real world to the grownups
And skip into a yellow field
Of flowers
Right up to my neck,
Perhaps if I wear my buttercup coloured jumper
They may not find me till next week!
I hope it doesn't rain
So I can lay here and look at the blue sky
Way up high
And if you wanted to come along
You could join me with your new picnic basket
And we would recite poetry
And eat Scotch eggs
And play "what if" games
And while the time away,
Till the cows come home
And how happy we would be
Swinging on a gate
Climbing over a stile
To see the new-born Easter lambs
Or perhaps inhale the coconutty smell of the gorse bush flowers
And I'd put daisies in your hair
And you can French plait mine
Like two girls at play
And if the others wanted to come too
They could,
But I would much rather it was just us two,
As long as we don't talk about anything grownup

Like deadlines, appointments, targets and Brexit.
We can just sit
And soak up the sunshine
While we dine
On the fruit and cheese
In this life of ease
We can jolly well do as we please!
Do say we can
And I'll meet you there
But mind you don't go without me
And together we'll be mellow
Just for the day
In our field of yellow.

Almost perfection

When my working day is done
I leave the town behind me and drive over the bridge
Casting my eye over to the right
On this peaceful night
I watch the last glimmer of the sun dancing on the ripples of the
little waves
And take in the scene as I do
Twice a day,
And wonder if I might take a drive to the beach
For a walk along the front
Or call in for a fish supper
Or maybe a roast
In one of the cosy little pubs along the way
The place is our own at this time of the year
When winter's sleep is slowly being shaken off
And the buds burst into life
Camellia, magnolia,
peach blossom,
As the bluebells start to raise shy heads
And the hawthorn dresses the lanes in white
But I turn off into my road
For it's not quite the same on your own,
I gather herbs for my supper
Something Italian I think,
And pour a ginger and rhubarb gin over lime and ice
Juniper berries for taste
And sit here with the cat on my lap
Another evening to waste:
It's beautiful here in the spring

Summer evenings are like the promise of a kiss
As the nights get longer and heady with the perfume of English roses
And I cannot sleep for the wonder of it,
And eventually drift away on a dream,
For there's magic here in the south
In our beautiful Devonshire
And it would almost be perfection if there was someone to share it with.

Just look up

When small-minded individuals treat you like a clown,
When the woes of the world try to bring you down
Tilt your head upwards
And look up!
When life's grind
makes your smile hard to find,
Unstrap that burden off your shoulders
Remember you are bolder
And infinitely better than this,
And you haven't even reached your full potential,
And to aim for the stars is essential;
Achieve those dreams
Never stop thinking about your plans and schemes
Keep looking above
That's where you'll find all the self-love
You need,
Stretch, breathe,
And between your belly and your head
Create a space,
Run that race
It's up to you to set the pace
Don't let them bring all their doom and gloom
Into that incredible room
You call your mind,
Let your horizons be broader
Than their infinitesimal little brains,
Let them threaten rain
And when the clouds gather
Look up

Way up,
Beyond the grey of this day
Into the blue yonder of your infinite headspace;
So what if they call you impractical, irrational, irresponsible
Better to be thus
Than boring!
Let them call you a dreamer
The one who goes off the beaten path
To look for the rarest flower,
Who climbs the hill
Just to look at the view
Never lose the wonder
That makes you YOU!
Leave them to their sepia colours
Yours encompasses the entire spectrum
Be the plectrum
That picks out the song
And you can never go wrong
Stand tall, stand strong
Lift your head high
Search for the blue in the sky
And your never need to ask why
Because you'll always be in luck
Just look up!!

Pink Gin summer

(Summer of 2019)

A day like today is too good to waste,
Drive to the coast in an open-topped sports car
With someone wonderful behind the wheel,
Leave it all behind
Feel the lure of the ocean as it draws us to it,
Meet up with friends
Outside in the sunshine,
Hold a large glass
of pink rhubarb gin
Swirl summer fruit in the bottom
While the fresh aroma of the botanicals hit your palate and nostrils,
Awaking the senses;
Walk hand in hand along the beach
Feel the overwhelming surge of gratitude for such a marvellous day,
Watch children splashing in the waves,
Collecting shells and pretty pebbles,
They have no care for tomorrow,
Feel the warmth on your shoulders
The happiness in your heart,
While your skin takes on the colour of autumn berries;
Eaton mess in big crystal bowls,
Fresh English strawberries,
Feel the colour of passion,
Breathe in the essence of new love,
Watch the butterflies dancing in the buddleia bush
And be like busy little bees finding sweetness everywhere
Take a chance on a dream;
And taste all the sweet nectar life has to offer,

The glue that binds us to each other;
Devon cream teas in friendly locally owned coffee shops,
Fish and chips by the sea,
Make each day count
Storing away the memories of blue skies days
For colder, darker skies
Go and watch the sunset as friends gather to let the good vibes
wash over them,
Eat freshly caught fish,
Barbecued by the water,
Feel the music, the movement, the moment,
As new friendships begin
We share stories,
Spend some time,
Summer and wine,
Time to ponder,
Time to wonder
New possibilities,
New opportunities,
This is what today is made for,
Open your door wide,
Go outside and find those beautiful things,
Meet those beautiful people
And don't look back with regret,
Perhaps just for today
It's time to forget.

Dear Lord

I'm tired but I'm trying,
It takes all my energy just to be positive, joyful, to keep going,
Dear Lord,
I have very little love in my life
But I'm trying to love those around me,
Even those who give very little back,
I'm trying to be a good friend,
I'm trying not to take it seriously
When no one calls and no one asks me how my day went,
When no one invites me out for a drink
I think of them and wish they would,
I would die for the love of those who really don't give me a second thought.
Dear Lord,
I'm trying to forgive those who are needlessly unkind,
The word that barbs,
The comment that makes me feel less than I am,
Less than I'm worth,
Perhaps they don't realise how much it bites?
Dear Lord,
I'm trying not to allow people I do not hold in high regard
Give me advice on my life,
Why does it matter so much?
Why does it hurt?
Dear Lord,
I am trying not to dwell on people who are neglectful of my feelings,
Who make promises and then break them,
Who think my time is valueless,
Like I don't count,

Like I don't need to rest.
Dear Lord,
I am trying to be patient
I don't wish any harm on anybody
Not even those who have wronged me,
Wounded my soul,
But karma is dragging her feet, Lord,
And injustice seems to be the winner here,
And the innocent suffer.
Dear Lord, I am mindful of the poor and I am grateful of all my blessings
But I'm tired, Lord,
And today is another day of hard toil,
When will I have time to just be,
When will I have time to be me?
To pursue my own wants, my own passions,
My creative spirit is drained
And I long to do more,
It's taking all my energy and all my will,
And yet it continues still.

The broken vase

I held the pieces in my hand,
This vessel that had once been a thing of great beauty
Laying in fragments now, discarded by its previous owner,
I wondered who could be so careless
Not to see its value,
To walk away
And not give it a second glance,
And I wanted to fix it
Restore it,
Mend and make good,
And so, it began,
Once piece at a time
With love and care
As the adhesive to hold it together,
And slowly this thing took shape,
And with each little effort
I stood back to admire its quality,
And when I was done
I placed it on the mantlepiece,
And I could hardly see a crack at all,
It would never hold water again,
Its fragile mould wouldn't stand the pressure,
But with careful handling would last my lifetime at least,
It was beautiful in spite of its imperfection,
And it made me think
We are all fatally flawed in one way or another,
Life has left its scars upon the surface
And deeper unseen holes in our souls,
And it wouldn't take much to send us toppling over the edge,

But all it takes is one loving hand to pull us from the abyss,
One kind word,
An apology for some wrong doing
Committed years ago
When we didn't know any better,
For we are all battered and broken
But beautiful nonetheless.

Journey's end

What brought me to this town?
Love?
Destiny?
A place to settle down?
To reinvent?
 In all the whole world
this is where I was sent,
This strange little town in south Devon,
Where the tidal waters wash the foreshore,
And then quietly take their leave once more,
It has its own beauty
Like a woman that wears many gowns,
She changes with the seasons,
Sometimes smiles, sometimes frowns,
At times you will find her
Magnolia sweet
When January wanders back this way,
And there is frost upon the street,
When we shield ourselves from the chills
Look up to the boughs and see shoots of green
For not too far away is Sister Spring
All green and serene,
Snow drops and daffodils
And little Narcissi
With heads shy bent,
And every May when the petals of the peach
Strew their blossom
Confetti blows around our feet.
And in the summer, there's no better place to be

Than beside the estuary
With an ice cream cone in hand
Or a pink gin on the edge of the creek
Where the boats harbour
And we gravitate looking for others to meet,
And there's happiness in the air
As we all forget our cares
And join in with the fair
And when carnival comes to town
And there's Stars in their Eyes,
And love wears many a disguise,
That's when the big boys and girls go out
And forget about work
For just one day and pass one night in happy play,
As we pray that summer will never go away,
The days are longer and we feel tanned and bronzed
And feel glad to be alive,
As we dream our dreams.
But when the leaves start to fall
And the damp sets in
And time slips back
As darkness seeps into the corners of our foggy brains,
How we retreat into our warm spaces
I, to my flat and my waiting little cat,
To ponder, to plan and sleep the long winter's night,
Sometimes the silence is so loud
It forces me to think,
I am no stranger to the loneliness of being by myself,
Boredom
Draws me back over the bridge
And into to the town

As I once more I long to seek
Friends who were once strangers to me,
What brought me here
To dwell with thee?
Kingsbridge?
Where's that to?
Like the waters that wash Bowcombe
Why is it that I always return to you?
For I was sent here
I was placed here
For what reason I cannot say
But I'm here now
So this is where I'll stay.

Ground Zero

It's a new week at ground zero
I'm still fatigued from the last,
One day of rest is never enough
So, as I reach for the vitamins and a cup of tea,
I pray I have the energy to get through to the other end of it,
Yet the sun is shining
And this is a week of new opportunities
And one mustn't be too glum
So put your best foot forward,
Leap into it with enthusiasm
And good intent,
Red lipstick and a splash of perfume will do the trick
To lift me out of the doldrums
And this fear of Monday morning.
Summer isn't over yet
And who knows what the day will bring?
Seize the moment, peeps!

A closing note

Let's lay the phantoms of the old year to rest
As the fire dies down
And the shadows fade and disappear
Sit down beside me
Let us reflect and give thanks
For all we have,
And remember those who didn't quite make it,
Let's pray for their souls to find peace
In the place beyond,
And for ourselves in this troubled world,
Let's light our candles
And send the light of hope out into the dark;
Forgive our enemies
And the people who spoke ill of us this past year
For they are just unhappy with themselves.
Let's give love to those who need it
And treasure and cherish
Those who held us high,
Forget the resentment
And the insecurities.
Leave the old baggage behind
Take it off your back
You don't need to carry it into to the new year
Bring only kindness
Only hope
Only love
And unburden yourself,
Share a little laughter
Give a warm smile

And take a break
once in a while
So you're not as thin as you want to be
And you don't have the latest car on the market,
But you have soul
And you are completely whole
And a little goes a long way
To brighten someone's day
Be brave
Be bold
You have another chance to make a difference
To make every day count.
Dazzle them with the brightness that shines from within
Don't let anyone spoil your sparkle
Reach out and be that sun
That warms everyone you see.
I wish you health and happiness
And a Happy New Year
With love from me.

... So please leave me to my dreams
        To my memories
            But most of all to my wish.
                Yes, I wanted to grow old in Africa,
                    but life had other horizons for
                        me to pursue.
                            Other things for me to do.